W9-CHX-463

THE BOOK OF
Little Hostas

THE BOOK OF
Little Hostas

200 Small, Very Small, and Mini Varieties

Kathy Guest Shadrack and Michael Shadrack
Consultant editor, Diana Grenfell

TIMBER PRESS
Portland · London

To our children—Jennifer, Vickie, Troy, and Emma
Four delightful young people

Frontispiece: A single miniature hosta, *H.* 'Cameo', in a terracotta pot, draped with a dwarf ivy. In these very small containers, there needs to be a strict watering regimen.

Published in 2010 by Timber Press, Inc.

The Haseltine Building
133 S.W. Second Avenue, Suite 450
Portland, Oregon 97204-3527
www.timberpress.com

2 The Quadrant
135 Salusbury Road
London NW6 6RJ
www.timberpress.co.uk

Printed in China
Text designed by Susan Applegate

Library of Congress Cataloging-in-Publication Data

Shadrack, Kathy Guest.
    The book of little hostas: 200 small, very small, and mini varieties/Kathy Guest Shadrack and Michael Shadrack; consultant editor, Diana Grenfell.—1st ed.
        p. cm.
    Includes bibliographical references and index.
    ISBN 978-1-60469-060-6
    1. Hosta—Varieties. 2. Miniature plants. I. Shadrack, Michael. II. Grenfell, Diana. III. Title.
    SB413.H73S53 2010
    635.9′3432—dc22   2010012436

Catalog records for this book are available from the Library of Congress and the British Library.

CONTENTS

PREFACE

Hostas have enjoyed great success, especially over the last twenty-five years, as a carefree, undemanding perennial of great diversity. There is a hosta for almost any site, and their sculptural beauty brings a bit of quiet sophistication to even the most exuberant flower garden.

Most of us are first drawn to large hostas. They make an imposing statement in the landscape and are often focal points; a magnificent *H.* 'Sum and Substance' or a well-grown *H.* 'Komodo Dragon' will catch the eye from across the garden. Most hosta collectors, too, begin with the larger plants. Then an evolution begins: as gardeners become more and more involved in collecting and growing the plants, they also become aware there exists a full spectrum of smaller hostas that mimic the shapes, colors, and textures of the larger hostas. There is every bit as much variety and variation in these garden gems, and it soon becomes clear that these smaller hostas can be as enthralling as the giants—and take up far less space and far less of the gardener's energy.

The smaller hostas have grown in popularity, especially over recent years, and it could be said that they now have almost a cult following. Hybridizers have taken notice, and more attention has been given to producing diminutive plants. The American Hosta Society (AHS) has also recognized the trend, not only by running a separate "mini hosta popularity poll" but also by establishing standards and definitions for small, very small, and miniature hostas.

Furthermore, as many of us no longer have the space or energy for a rolling garden, we turn to a more manageable space: a raised bed, a trough, or even a collection of potted plants on a deck or patio. Smaller hostas are perfectly suited to this focused kind of gardening. They add texture, color, and excitement in a confined area.

Little hostas, however, do take specialized care and siting in order to be grown optimally. The purpose of this book is to introduce you, the reader, to the palette of these small, very small, and miniature hostas, address how to grow them to perfection, and offer ideas on how to best use them in the garden, in containers, and as specimens. We hope that you find something in this book to stimulate, titillate, or otherwise encourage you to grow some little hostas, start a new collection, or create a landscape in miniature. We hope you might learn something new, or be stirred to learn more about one aspect or another touched upon here. If we do that, we have met our goal.

Acknowledgements

We would like first to thank Diana Grenfell, who unselfishly and generously provided the opportunity for this book, and then offered her total and absolute support so that we could accomplish it. As consultant editor, she has freely shared her experience and expertise, her eyes and criticism, her hard work and her enthusiasm. Diana has been a hosta champion to many, but to us she has also been a very special mentor and friend. There are no words that can adequately express our appreciation to her.

We appreciate Anna Mumford, our commissioning editor from Timber Press, who had confidence in our abilities, and we thank her for the clear and expert advice she gave us throughout the writing process.

We would like to thank Warren Pollock, who has spent many hours vetting—and sometimes debating—most of the chapters. We are grateful for his exceptional knowledge, practiced proofreading, and patience.

W. George Schmid has been wonderful and also exceptionally patient in explaining the intricacies of the species, endeavoring to keep us as correct as possible. He helped us to understand the "roots" of the smaller hostas.

Bob Solberg offered key assistance and advice about the nuances of growing small hostas well. He spent a great deal of time reading what we had written and then challenging the parts that needed challenging.

As well as the help and support we have received, we have tried to keep track of two years' worth of photo opportunities, advice, gardens, quotes, and chance conversations. Our deep and humble appreciation to all those hosta friends, around the world, who gave us unrestricted access to their gardens and their knowledge, with special thanks to Tony Avent, Bob Bauer, Doug Beilstein, Sandra Bond, Ann and Roger Bowden, Carol Brashear, John Coble, Peter Cross and Oscar Cross, Walter Cullerton, C. H. Falstad, Marco and Joyce Fransen, Mike and Libby Greanya, Hans Hansen, Jack Hirsch, Jerry Kral, Bob Kuk, Mark Langden, Gary Lindheimer, Ran and Katie Lydell, Bill Meyer, Dick O'Melay, Al Pfieffer, Hugo Philips, Kevin Plumley, Peter and Jean Ruh, Tim Saville, Carolyn Schaffner, Bill Silvers, Nancy Solberg, Van and Shirley Wade, Kevin Walek, Cynthia Wilhoite, Jim and Sandy Wilkins, and Mark Zilis.

Hosta venusta, one of the first small species
hostas introduced to gardeners.

CHAPTER ONE

A Brief Introduction to Hostas

WHEN MOST PEOPLE THINK of hostas, what springs to mind are majestic plants with luxuriant leaves anchoring a shady corner of the garden. It still surprises some gardeners that hostas come in a myriad of sizes, and that small, very small, and miniature hostas are equally valuable, charming, and exciting when properly set in small spaces.

Hostas are clump-forming perennials, generally grown for their impressive foliage. Originating from Japan, China, and Korea, they first crossed to the West in the late 1700s, in the form of seeds collected from the sweetly fragrant flowers of *H. plantaginea* (August lily). Philipp von Siebold, Robert Fortune, most probably Thomas Hogg, and other early collectors introduced hostas to Europe and the United States during the plant collecting frenzy of the 1800s. These early hostas are still grown, although in some cases they offer little as decorative garden plants other than durability and dependability.

This is, after all, the great charm of hostas. As a genus, they are undemanding garden plants. Few pests bother them, with the notable exception of slugs and snails. Although shade-tolerant, they are not shade-loving. They are often thought to thrive in the darkest, driest parts of the garden. In fact, they do better in dappled shade, some even preferring some sun. They will persist, however, and have been the backbone of gardens worldwide for over a century.

W. George Schmid, respected hosta author and researcher of the genus, refers to several clumps of the huge-leafed *H. sieboldiana* planted by his grandfather prior to 1900, which still thrive. Most American heritage gardens include *Hh. sieboldiana*, *plantaginea*, and the diminutive *venusta*. In the United Kingdom, illustrious plantswoman and designer Gertrude Jekyll featured hostas in pots for drama, as well as including them as complementary plants and accents in her legendary gardens. Her contemporary William Robinson, one of the first exponents of wilder gardens, used them in different but equally attractive settings. More *Hosta* species began to arrive in the West; these were grown in botanic gardens and public spaces, mostly as groundcover, creating little interest. But things were to change.

On the eastern seaboard of the United States, landscape designer and plantswoman Mrs. Frances Williams became an avid hosta collector and, always keen for something new or different, quite by chance spotted a yellow margin on a single hosta in a row of glaucous blue *H. sieboldiana* 'Elegans' at Bristol Nurseries, in Connecticut. Mrs. Williams generously passed pieces of her new plant to various individuals and nurseries in her locality, where it was known by several different names. The hosta was eventually sent to Oxford Botanic Garden in the United Kingdom, well known for its collection of variegated plants, where the superintendent, George Robinson, named it in her honor during a lecture at the prestigious Royal Horticultural Society Halls in London. *Hosta* 'Frances Williams' immediately became a sensation, which did much to bring hostas to the attention of the gardening public, and the flower arranging movement. Before long, pure yellow-leafed sports of this plant were noticed in several countries, thus creating even more interest and enthusiasm for the plant.

Eric Smith, a British plantsman, during his employment as a propagator for the renowned English nursery, Hilliers of Winchester in the 1960s and early '70s, took a liking to hostas and raised a deep blue-leafed seedling from Robert Fortune's *H.* 'Tokudama', eventually named *H.* 'Buckshaw Blue'. He then began hybridizing in earnest from the still-limited range of hostas available. Eric's main ambition was to raise a series of smaller blue-leafed hostas more suited to gardeners with less space. A chance crossing of *H.* 'Tardiflora' with an unusually late-flowering *H. sieboldiana* 'Elegans Alba' produced his desired aim, *H.* 'Blue Moon'; and *H.* 'Halcyon', his best-known introduction, remains high on hosta popularity polls.

During his time at Buckshaw Gardens and The Plantsman Nursery with Jim Archibald, and later as head gardener at nearby Hadspen House, Eric began a quest to raise yellow-leafed

Hosta 'Blue Moon', one of the smallest varieties produced by plantsman Eric Smith.

hostas whose color held for the whole season. Quite soon he was overtaken in this endeavor, but one of the smaller plants he worked on was the vivid yellow-centered green-margined cultivar of *H. sieboldii*, 'Kabitan', from which he raised the chrome yellow--leafed *H.* 'Golden Oriole'. American hosta fancier Russ O'Harra, working on the same lines, saw the potential of the pale yellow-leafed *H. sieboldii* f. *subchrocea*, and over a decade introduced many small and miniature yellow-leafed hostas, including *H.* 'Feather Boa', *H.* 'Gingee', and *H.* 'Ground Sulphur'. Both Buckshaw Gardens and Hadspen House became the "Holy Grail" for hosta collectors traveling from America and Europe, as well as a favorite haunt of keen gardeners in Britain. A longstanding friendship between Eric Smith and Alex Summers, America's hosta pioneer, was forged, with the result that American hosta breeders soon had access to a wider variety of hostas from which to raise new and more exciting introductions.

In the early days of hosta collecting in the United States, one nursery stands out, not only for its longevity but for its many hosta introductions that grace our gardens today. This is Savory Gardens of Edina, Minnesota, founded in 1946 by Robert Savory and now operated by his son, Dennis. From Savory came some of the best-known and -loved small hostas, including *H.* 'Golden Tiara', which spawned a "dynasty" (see chapter six), and *H.* 'Tiny Tears', one of the smallest of the miniature hostas, registered in 1977.

A frequent visitor to nurseries in Japan, Paul Aden, collector and breeder of a huge number of hostas, was another forerunner in the introduction of miniature hostas to the market. He had access to the tiniest species, *Hh. gracillima, pulchella,* and *venusta.* From *H.*

Hosta 'Feather Boa', one of the first small yellow varieties.

Hosta 'Tiny Tears', one of the smallest hosta varieties.

Hosta 'Tet-A-Poo'

pulchella came the glossy leafed *H.* 'Shining Tot'; and he used his smallish *H.* 'Blue Cadet' to produce thicker and bluer leaves in his diminutive hostas, of which *H.* 'Tet-A-Poo' and *H.* 'Tot Tot' are among the best.

An important event that raised the profile of the hosta was the formation in 1968 of the American Hosta Society, an organization of hosta enthusiasts who share information as well as acting as a resource for learning about hostas. As interest in hostas grew, enthusiasts, hybridizers, and collectors began to form local groups. Today membership in the AHS is worldwide, and several other international hosta societies exist. The AHS also encompasses an active online community of hosta admirers and a recently formed Mini Hosta Forum (see "Further Reading") devoted to growing and sharing information on the smaller hostas.

Intense interest in smaller hostas, although always an undercurrent among collectors, was ignited by the 1996 introduction of *H.* 'Pandora's Box'. This sport of *H.* 'Baby Bunting' with a crisp white center and a wide, feathered blue-green margin became an instant "must have" on every collector's list. So an interest, once created, must be satisfied. In 2008 alone, twenty-six new small and miniature hostas were registered, representing almost 17 percent of all hostas registered that year, and many others not yet formally registered are on the market.

Clearly, little hostas are a growing trend.

Hosta 'Pandora's Box'

A collection of small potted hostas, together with larger examples, in the garden of Warren and Ali Pollock.

CHAPTER TWO

It's a Small World After All

THE WORLD OF SMALL and miniature hostas is a new and exciting one. It's true that for a bold statement in the shade garden, bigger is better; there are, however, many very good reasons for looking beyond the super-sized. Displaying all the variation in leaf shape, texture, and color of the larger plants, little hostas are delightful in a tight city lot or townhouse garden. They do well on windowsills and in containers, arranged in tiers on steps for an artistic effect. They can join miniature trees and dwarf conifers to form a diminutive landscape, or they can be arranged with small ornaments and figurines in a fairy garden.

What is a little hosta?

"I know it when I see it." So famously wrote Justice Potter Stewart, declining to specifically define pornography. The same might be said for little hostas. Over the years, the terms "small," "dwarf," "tiny," and "miniature" were used loosely to describe smaller hostas. In an effort to make the terms meaningful, especially with the enormous popularity these little plants now enjoy, the American Hosta Society worked out definitions based upon the leaf blade area for small and mini hostas (and

discontinued the terms "dwarf" and "tiny"). Diana Grenfell, noted British author and hosta authority, then crafted a third, in-between category, "very small," to encompass those hostas larger than a mini but still quite small and requiring specialized care. "Small," the next AHS category larger in size than "mini," was so broad that there was a visual gap between the two classifications; the new "very small" category, introduced in *The New Encyclopedia of Hostas* (the revised edition of *The Color Encyclopedia of Hostas*), bridged that gap. The present categories, as defined, are as follows:

"Small"

SMALL HOSTA: Leaf blade area greater than about 10 square inches but less than about 25 square inches. (The upper limit is roughly 5×5 in., but most are closer to 3×5 in.) Mature clump height usually ranges from 10 inches to about 15 inches.
EXAMPLES: *H.* 'Golden Tiara', *H.* 'Emerald Tiara'
USES: Most hostas in the "small" category are vigorous enough for garden planting, as long as care is taken that they are not overwhelmed by nearby larger plants.

"Smaller"

VERY SMALL HOSTA: Leaf blade area greater than about 4 square inches but less than about 10 square inches, with a leaf blade length of under about 6 inches. (Most are approximately 3 × 3 in.) Mature clump height usually ranges from 6 inches to about 10 inches.

EXAMPLES: *H.* 'Baby Bunting', *H.* 'Masquerade'

USES: Some especially vigorous cultivars may be suitable for the garden, but most are better in a special planting area.

"Smallest"

MINIATURE (MINI) HOSTA: Leaf blade area of about 4 square inches or less and a leaf blade no longer than about 4.5 inches. (Visualize an upper limit of 2 × 2 in., not including the petiole.) Mature clump height is usually less than about 6 inches.

EXAMPLES: *H.* 'Tiny Tears', *H.* 'Daisy Doolittle'

USES: Primarily container plants, or in an especially prepared section of the garden.

It should be noted that the definitions as provided are intended for categorizing hostas in catalogs, plant lists, and hosta shows, but they do not necessarily consider the growth habit of the plant. There are hostas that may fit the leaf criteria, yet their growth habit is not as conveniently restrained. For example, a hosta may meet the leaf size for "mini" yet have a petiole (leaf stem) length that will cause it to overwhelm a trough garden. Or a hosta may have

Hosta 'Masquerade'

a "very small" leaf size, yet the plant grows in a sprawling manner, with the end result being a hosta that can spread to 3 feet across—hardly what is needed when planning a display in a small area.

In this book, taking into account the overall plant in addition to the leaf size, we consider "little" any hosta that will grow no higher than about 12 inches and no wider than about 24 inches. It should be noted that, very broadly speaking, the smaller the hosta, the more exacting the cultural requirements. One that immediately springs to mind is *H.* 'Uzu-no-mai', a diminutive hosta that has spread heart-break among growers, although a few dedicated souls have been able to keep it alive by careful container planting and very special care. There are other tiny hostas, conversely,

Hosta 'Daisy Doolittle', a miniature hosta less than 6 inches high.

Hosta 'Little Wonder', *H.* 'Faithful Heart', *H.* 'Kifukurin Ko Mame', and *H.* 'Stiletto' planted together in a collection of small hostas.

that will flourish despite your best attempts to send them to plant heaven; *H. pulchella* is one such.

On the upper end of the spectrum are the "larger small" hostas (an oxymoron, like jumbo shrimp) that are generally as carefree as their full-sized brethren and will coast along quite happily in the garden with a regimen of benign neglect. *Hosta* 'Golden Tiara', *H.* 'Emerald Tiara', *H.* 'Blue Mouse Ears', *H.* 'Twist of Lime', and *H.* 'Vera Verde' are examples of plants suitable for the garden without special care. *Hosta* 'Hope' and other minis require more careful attention.

Smaller *Hosta* species

Where do smaller hostas come from? To answer this, we must refer back to the beginning—the smallest of the species. Hostas are, first of all, wild plants from Japan, China, and Korea, where they have grown for eons. These wild plants are species. As W. George Schmid writes, "Biological species are defined as populations of similar individuals, alike in structural and functional characteristics, which in nature breed only with each other, and which have a common heritage (i.e., they are genetically closely related). *Hosta* species can and do interbreed (in most cases) resulting in populations that are intergrading (interspecific) hybrid swarms. Only geographic isolation will keep *Hosta* species from hybridizing in nature. For this reason, the biological definition is rarely applied to the genus *Hosta*." Instead, when we refer to a *Hosta* species, we mean that to be the "principal basic rank" of a genus.

All the hosta cultivars now grown have arisen from populations growing in the wild.

They are all perennial plants, enjoying a period of winter dormancy, but they come from very diverse geographical areas and have adapted to a range of climatic conditions. Some grow on craggy cliffs, others in deep isolated valleys. Some hostas can be found on grassy plains, others on mountaintops. There are hostas growing in boggy areas, and hostas growing in woods and forests. The species hostas are diverse in size, shape, and growth patterns, and even populations of the same species can vary significantly.

While species hostas may not be popular garden plants, they are important because they have been used extensively by hosta hybridizers to produce some of our most garden-worthy cultivars; and recently these hybrids and the species behind them have produced some excellent sports. It is helpful to know which species may lurk in a hosta's background in order to provide it with optimum growing conditions. The following is a selection of the small species hostas that figure most prominently in currently available cultivars.

Hosta gracillima
SMALL ROCK HOSTA

This species forms a very low, dense mound of small green foliage with medium-purple flowers in early autumn. The leaves are shaped like an elongated teardrop and have a slightly rippled margin. Especially suited to trough and rock garden planting. Cultivars arising from *H. gracillima* include *H.* 'Little Wiggler', *H.* 'Sugar Plum Fairy', and *H.* 'Vera Verde'.

Hosta longipes
ROCK HOSTA

This species forms a small to medium mound. Leaves are shiny mid- to dark green, a flat oval with a slight wave and deep, distinct veining. Pale purple flowers occur in late summer to autumn. This hosta and its progeny require ample water with sharp drainage and some protection from summer sun. Notable cultivars include *H.* 'Dim Sum', *H.* 'Fire Island', and *H. longipes* 'Ogon Amagi'.

Hosta longissima

Hosta 'Bitsy Gold', a *H. longissima* hybrid.

Hosta longissima
SWAMP HOSTA

Adapted to open grassy swamp-land, this species requires more water than others. *Hosta longissima* var. *longifolia* has rhizomatous root structures, which cause it to spread, and long, narrow, strappy leaves. *Hosta longissima* var. *brevifolia*, the far more common type, has shorter leaves and grows in a dense mound of arching foliage. Cultivars with *H. longissima* in the background include *H.* 'Bitsy Green', *H.* 'Bitsy Gold', and *H.* 'Purple Lady Fingers'.

Hosta minor

This species originated in Korea, where it inhabits mountains, misty regions with high rainfall. The plant forms a small, spreading mound, profusely flowering in midsummer. Leaves are oval with a curved tip, arching and slightly folded. *Hosta minor* and *H. venusta* share a common ancestor, which has resulted in both hostas having unique parallel ridges along the flower scape (evident by running the tip of your tongue along the scape).

Hosta nakaiana

Another Korean species that figures prominently in the background of many hostas, including the Tiara Series. This species is a vigorous grower and profuse flowerer. Leaves are heart-shaped, and the plant forms a spreading mound. It and its progeny grow best in moist, dappled shade.

Hosta pulchella

Originating in Japan, where it is found high in the mountains, growing in rock fissures, this rhizomatous species forms a tiny mound of shiny dark green, elongated heart-shaped leaves, slightly wavy and arching, with good substance. The medium-purple flowers form in early summer. *Hosta pulchella* is the smallest of all *Hosta* species. Notable cultivars include *H.* 'Kifukurin Ubatake', *H.* 'Shining Tot', and *H.* 'Stiletto'.

Hosta 'Tot Tot', a variety from the *H. venusta* line.

Hosta venusta

One of the smallest and perhaps the most influential species, *H. venusta* is used in dozens of breeding programs and has produced many worthy hybrids and sports. It grows only to about 6 inches high, forming a dense mound of teardrop-shaped green leaves. Blooms midsummer. *Hosta venusta* comes from mountainous areas, where it grows between rocks in shady areas; its offspring should therefore enjoy a location on a rockery, provided there is plenty of room for deep-growing roots. Certain *H. venusta* cultivars (*H.* 'Cody', *H.* 'Striker', *H.* 'Tiny Tears', *H.* 'Tot Tot') are especially good for rock gardens; others include *H.* 'Thumb Nail', *H.* 'Gosan Gold Midget', and *H.* 'Masquerade'.

Hosta laevigata

Hosta yingeri

Hosta laevigata
Hosta yingeri

These two small species were recently discovered among rocks on isolated islands, where they enjoy deep but restricted root growth and heavy rainfall. It is anticipated that both will pass on their thick substance, glossy leaves, and spidery flowers to future sports and hybrids. *Hosta* 'Ray of Hope' is an example.

Why little hostas?

With changing lifestyles and the shrinking of both properties and available hours and energy to spend tending a garden, being able to create just as much pleasure and diversity of color and form in a confined space is appealing. In fact, in many ways, small-scale gardens are even better. It's satisfying to have a garden where such chores as weeding and watering can be tended to quickly. What's more, the downsizing of plant material is occurring not just with hosta breeders but across the horticultural spectrum—mini roses and astilbes, dwarf Japanese maples and conifers, pocket-sized ferns—with new breakthroughs in smaller versions of other garden staples introduced each year. As a result, those of us who prefer variety in the garden have a wide selection of plants that will fit in nicely with our small and mini hostas.

Landscaping with smaller hostas requires that the surroundings be to scale. This fact alone suggests economy of energy as well as cost. A gardener does not need to hire a front-end loader to move boulders around when the same effect can be created in a fraction of the space with materials that can be positioned by hand. A classic combination of rock, conifer, and hosta can be displayed in a trough instead of commanding a major part of the garden.

An early landscape treatment that we often recall was a tableau a friend created under the boughs of a large fir tree. Featured were several small hostas, a tiny bridge, and a gravel stream. One felt transported, as though looking through the wrong end of a telescope. This secret garden in miniature lit a passion for dwarfed plants that ultimately has led to this book.

A collection of little hostas with Japanese statuary.

Hosta 'Woodland Elf', *H.* 'Hope', *H.* 'Baby Blue Eyes', and *H.* 'Cheesecake' planted in a small trough with a miniature spruce.

Smaller hostas are more often appreciated for overall effect rather than as part of the larger garden, and in fact there are some aspects particular to the smaller plants that are not much seen in the larger varieties. For example, some growers have concentrated their efforts on little hostas with extremely narrow, rippled leaves. The effect is electrifying, as the plant aspect is one of intense movement and energy (as in *H.* 'Roller Coaster Ride' and *H.* 'X-Rated'). There is another set of little hostas with twisty, upright foliage (*H.* 'Apple Court', *H.* 'Tongue Twister', *H.* 'Little Stiffy'). Again, the overall appearance of the lone hosta creates the effect.

When there isn't space, time, or energy for a large garden, you can replicate the same shapes, colors, textures, and mood on a small scale.

Part of a miniature garden that includes *Hosta* 'Striker', *H.* 'Elsley Runner', and *H.* 'Tot Tot'.

A group of small hostas with different leaf colors and patterns planted in a raised bed.

CHAPTER THREE

How to Grow and Care For Your Little Hostas

ALTHOUGH HOSTAS AS GARDEN PLANTS are thought to be carefree, the very small and miniature hostas sometimes require a little more care. The larger of the little plants, such as *H.* 'Golden Tiara' or *H.* 'Lakeside Dragonfly', are garden-worthy and will require no special treatment beyond that you would give any treasured plant—attention to watering and weeding. Broadly speaking, the smaller the hosta, the slightly more demanding the culture. The tiniest hostas with large areas of white on their leaves can be particularly tricky but well worth the effort.

Soil

The smaller the hosta, the more important the soil mixture in which it is planted. Larger hostas can tolerate and even thrive in almost any kind of soil (with the possible exceptions of soggy clay and pure beach sand), but little hostas are more finicky and will grow best in a slightly acidic/ericaceous soil that drains well. We have been impressed by how easily little hostas grew in gardens where the soil is quite sandy; however, the rest of us will need to give some attention to the growing media in order to give our hostas the best chance for optimum growth.

Soil texture is a reflection of the mineral content in a soil. Soil high in gravel will feel gritty; soil composed of silt will feel like flour; and clay soil, with the smallest particles of all, will feel sticky and dries to virtual cement. Spending time on creating good soil will vastly improve your success with the tiniest and most difficult of these plants, and will make any hosta in your collection grow to its full potential. A perfect soil mixture for small hostas will keep roots moist, drain very well, and include tiny air pockets to allow oxygen to reach their roots. The antithesis for small hostas is a soggy clay, too dense and compacted for delicate roots.

A good planting mix will contain 50 percent good quality native garden soil, 25 percent organic matter, and 25 percent particulate, or solid and inert particles. What is considered good quality native garden soil? If you are gifted with sandy loam, every gardener's dream soil, you are already there. Most of us, however, do not have the perfect soil in our garden and will need to bring in bagged or loose soil as our base. Our own garden has an evil mixture of very heavy clay over shale, which doesn't drain in the least; all our gardens are, therefore, raised to some degree.

And if you are planting containers or a small area, it's probably best to start with commercially bagged soil. Good-quality bagged soil is available, and it is worth paying a little more in order to start with a better quality.

Customized, bagged soil-less blends are usually available through horticultural wholesalers. In the United States, some of the larger and best-known brands include Fafard, Metro-Mix, and ProMix; a search of these brands will lead you to a local supplier. In the United Kingdom, popular brands are Levington or Scotts. The key elements to look for in a bagged mix are a pH of 6.0 to 5.5, some form of particulate to promote drainage, and an organic component (peat moss, composted bark) for the remainder. Most bagged mixes will contain perlite and/or vermiculite to lighten the mix. These light-colored particles do improve drainage, but the perlite especially resembles tiny pieces of Styrofoam. Perlite is actually a sterile material produced by super-heating volcanic rock, resulting in a very lightweight, porous material; its principal value in soil mixtures is aeration, but because it is so light it often floats to the surface of the soil over time and looks unsightly. You may find the resulting confetti look to be a distraction.

When creating your own planting mix, in addition to the soil base, add some good amendments.

Recommended amendments

• Triple-ground or composted pine bark is a mixture of very small bark chips along with partially decomposed bark, resembling peat. This particular product may even be used alone in a pot, if you wish; however, it should be noted that as the bark continues to decompose, there may be some nitrogen depletion, and the mix will lose some of its excellent drainage properties. If you choose to use this product alone, a small amount of high-nitrogen fertilizer may be added, and your plant should be examined each spring and repotted as necessary.

• Coir, or coconut dust, is an alternative to peat moss as a soil amendment. Peat moss is a product of decomposed plant material, sphagnum moss, in bogs over hundreds of years; it holds moisture in the soil and improves soil texture or tilth. There is a concern, however, that peat is virtually a non-renewable resource and that responsible gardeners should use alternatives when possible. Coir is a good alternative; it retains some moisture, although not as well as peat, and improves soil texture. Unlike peat, however, it is pH neutral and decomposes at a much slower rate. It is also easily produced and replenished. The downside is that coir may not be as readily available everywhere.

• Compost (composted vegetable and garden waste) has moisture-retaining properties and is high in organic matter. It will improve soil texture and tilth and add nutrients to your soil. Every gardener should find a place for a small pile of organic waste and regularly add coffee grounds, eggshells, vegetable peels, grass clippings, and chopped leaves. Composting, however, takes time and attention to work properly.

All organic components will decompose over time. You will need to refresh your mixture periodically, especially for container-grown plants, as the breakdown will cause your mix to lose the desirable soil structure and become compacted. A compacted soil will not drain properly and roots will suffer.

Particulates

Drainage (of which more later) is extremely important when crafting a soil mix for your little hostas. The higher the particulate/grit content, the less the chance that your hosta will become waterlogged. As important as moisture is to hostas, they cannot tolerate soggy soil, and for the smallest plants, this becomes critical. A good balanced mix will keep tiny roots evenly moist but never wet. The addition of a particulate or grit to the soil will allow for minute spaces in your soil mix through which water can drain and oxygen can reach roots.

Recommended particulates

• Builder's sand. Available from building supply stores. Despite the name, this is not sand but a fine gravel and grit, used for concrete. Add it to your mixture by the handful until the result feels rough to the touch.

• Turkey grit. Available from feed stores. This is a feed additive for large poultry and can be composed of crushed oyster shells, granite, or limestone. Granite is preferred since it will not react with the planting media. Make sure you ask for turkey grit and not poultry grit, a much finer grind intended for smaller birds.

• Turface. A commercial product intended for athletic fields. Turface is hard-fired clay particles resembling kitty litter which provide drainage without decomposing. It also has some moisture-retaining properties.

• Grape pomace. In wine-producing areas, this by-product, composed of skin and seeds, is readily available and has both organic as well as particulate properties. One local hosta grower in our area buys pomace mixed with composted manure and claims that his hostas actively crave it. His amended soil is so beautifully friable that he is able to dig a plant with his bare hands.

• Coffee grounds. Spent coffee grounds are readily available in quantity from your local coffee shop and offer organic as well as drainage benefits. The grounds will also keep the pH of your soil on the lower side. Additionally, a study conducted by the Department of Agriculture in Hilo, Hawaii, suggests there may be a side benefit to using coffee grounds in that they adversely affect your local slug population. This study has since been disputed, but coffee grounds are a good soil additive regardless.

What to do with your new hostas

Your new hostas may arrive potted, newly divided from a friend, or (when mail ordering) bare root. They should be treated differently, depending upon the category into which they fall.

If you have received your hosta as an established potted plant, you need not do anything immediately except to put the pot in a bright but shaded area; and make sure to water when the soil seems dry, probably every other day.

Most mail-order hostas will arrive bare root, meaning the plant will come with no soil and may be wrapped in barely moist paper towel. When purchasing little hostas bare root, we recommend soaking them overnight to rehydrate and then potting until the plant is established. If you receive the plant bare root later in the year, you may even wish to hold them over in a container until the following spring, when growth begins, before transferring the plant to its final spot in your garden.

A newly divided hosta will need a bit of tender loving care. If the plant seems to be suffering—leaves droopy or yellowing—you will need to be especially vigilant until it has recovered. Remove the yellowed leaves (in fact, don't be afraid to cut back all the leaves), pot in a free-draining soil mix, and water every other day for a couple of weeks. If the roots appear to be dry, an overnight soaking in a bucket of water prior to planting will help it to recover.

If you receive mail-order plugs, or plants not too long out of tissue culture, they will need even slightly different care and attention. It is a good idea to not only plant these plugs into a container immediately, but to keep the container which holds them very near the house so that a close eye can be kept on them. These plants have been growing under controlled conditions, and so watering is important until they are adjusted.

Planting your hostas

Planting hostas is easy. In fact, we often tell people to dig a hole, drop the plant in, and get out of the way, but that may be a little over-simplified. Small, very small, and mini hostas should be planted as you would any other hosta, but perhaps with a little more care. Your hosta will respond well if you keep a few tips and tricks in mind. It helps to understand that small hostas have fine, shallow roots, which can dry out quickly. Competition from tree

roots complicates the situation further (more on this, later), and they cannot withstand drought as well as their deeper-rooted brethren. It is important that soil around little hostas not be compacted so that their delicate roots are able to function fully to supply the plant with water and nutrients.

If you are transferring a hosta from one pot to another, you will be unlikely to encounter problems. The new container should be only slightly larger, both in diameter and depth, than the original. Carefully tip out the plant, and note whether it appears to be root bound (a situation that occurs when a plant remains for too long in the same pot and the roots, having nowhere to go, become matted and circle the inside of the pot). If a plant is found in this condition, the receiving pot will need to be even larger.

A potted hosta will have exhausted the soil in its old pot and so, for the occasion of moving to a new one, why not replenish the soil as well? Shake off as much of the old soil as possible; if the plant is root bound, a Phillips screwdriver is a good tool for gently prying apart roots and releasing some more of the soil without causing damage. You don't need to bare root—you simply are preparing the plant for the receiving pot in the best possible way. Plant the hosta at same depth as it was in the previous pot. Add the tired old soil to your garden or to your compost pile.

If you have received a divided hosta or bare root plant, and intend to pot it, the procedure is this. Select a pot slightly wider and deeper than the root spread. Fill the bottom of the container with your planting medium, then build a mound in the center so that the area looks like a reverse donut. Seat your hosta on

Part of Diana Grenfell's National Plant Collection in a raised bed in her garden at Newnham-on-Severn, Gloucestershire, England.

the mound, spreading the roots around it like a party dress, out and downward. Build your mound up or down to make sure the plant is not too shallow or too deep, and then backfill with your planting medium, tamping gently as you go, so that the crown of the plant (the area where the roots and leaves join) lies just below the soil surface. Water so that the soil settles, and top up with more soil.

The same goes for planting in the garden. First improve the soil so that it is as light and permeable as reasonable. Dig a hole larger than the spread of the roots, then follow the procedure just given for planting in a pot. You should water the plant in thoroughly, and add more soil where necessary. Keep watering every other day for two to three weeks, at which time the plant should be established.

Try to plant your last hostas no later than six weeks before the first frost date in order to give them an opportunity to harden off. The problem with late planting, especially for the little hostas in colder climates, is that the freezing and thawing of the ground can cause the hosta to heave, a condition where the crown loses contact with the soil. Sometimes, the plant is actually spat out like an orange seed and left lying on top of the ground, but usually it winds up standing on its roots. Either way, the end product is a desiccated crown and dead plant in the spring. If you have a potted hosta that didn't get planted, you can sink the entire pot into the ground for the winter, and the plant won't know that it didn't get planted.

Mulching

Adding a light mulch will help your new hosta in several ways: it helps conserve moisture in your planting mix; it offers some protection from weather extremes; and, especially with the smallest hostas, it prevents soil from splashing up on tiny leaves during a heavy rain, spoiling the appearance and reducing the plant's ability to process chlorophyll. Mulching a mini or very small hosta is especially important. At the upper end of the "small scale," plants will accept a standard mulch, such as shredded bark, or even wood chips (always remember to keep these types of mulch away from the crown of the plant, where it may encourage rot or vermin). But the smaller hostas will look better if care is taken to match the scale of your mulch to the size of the plant. *Hosta* 'Tiny Tears' will be lost in a sea of bark, but careful selection of your mulch will set off the plant while offering the protection it needs. Mulches we have seen or used ourselves include the following sorts of inorganic, organic, and living mulches.

Inorganic mulches

• Pea gravel. A very small-sized smooth gravel, usually in shades of tan and gray. The gravel should be washed first to dispense with any dust and then arranged in a thin layer around your hostas.

• Aquarium gravel. Available in many colors and may have either a shiny or dull sheen. Black gravel is especially dramatic for any colored plant, and blue or blue-green shades are effective in showing off a yellow-leafed hosta. Again, the mulch layer does not need to be deep, but rather just hide the soil.

• Sea glass and polished stone. Although the size might be slightly larger, the look is refined and pleasing in containers. When using this type of mulch, you need not absolutely cover the underlying soil. This type of mulch is fabulous when watering as well, since the hard surface breaks the force of the stream.

• Gray slate chips and marble chips. Chips of slate laid carefully and overlapping are not only a restful and refined mulch, they can be arranged to suggest a stream flowing through the hosta bed. Marble chips are another possibility and, depending upon the color of marble used, can be arranged to contrast with or complement your hosta collection.

Organic mulches

• Cocoa shells or buckwheat hulls will retain more water than an inorganic mulch but still maintain scale. Cocoa shells are the byproduct of chocolate processing and are a deep

Small hostas mulched with a layer of pea gravel in the garden of Mike and Libby Greanya, Jackson, Michigan.

brown color. They give off a pleasing, faint "chocolate brownie" aroma after a rain. They may also grow a fungus in humid weather, but it seems to do no harm, and a stirring of the shells will remedy the situation. Buckwheat hulls are sometimes used in pillows or yoga mats and have no particular odor. Both products, being organic, will break down fairly quickly and improve soil texture. If you have concerns about nitrogen depletion as a result of the decomposition, you may add a small amount of high-nitrogen fertilizer to the top layer. The problem with both shells and hulls is that they are very light when dry and can easily blow away. A sprinkling with the hose will keep them in place.

• Pine bark fines (also called ground pine bark or pine soil conditioner) are small enough to maintain scale and are a pleasing chestnut color. You may wish to sieve out the smallest particles and add those to your soil mixture.

Hosta 'Dragon Tails', like any bright yellow hosta, contrasts well against a mulch of gray slate chips.

Living mulches

• Small hostas can also work well with a living mulch, a polite groundcover. By "polite," we mean one that is not aggressive (avoid English ivy, pachysandra, myrtle, and ajuga).

• Creeping thyme (*Thymus serpyllum*) works well as a groundcover, especially if your drainage is fairly sharp. It has the additional advantage of fragrance.

• Golden creeping Jenny (*Lysimachia nummularia* 'Aurea') grows prostrate in a loose mat and will also gracefully trail over a rock wall or container. The golden color of its small round yellow leaves is particularly effective with blue hostas.

• Moss (many varieties—common fern moss is probably best). Moss tolerates the most moisture in the soil. When established, it will form a velvety carpet in the garden, or act as

Hosta 'Little Jay', newly planted and treated with a dark mulch of pine bark fines.

a feathery foil in a container. Moss can, however, overwhelm a very small or miniature hosta, so pinch it away if it gets too close.

• Moss phlox (*Phlox subulata*) will appreciate more moisture than creeping thyme or golden creeping Jenny but will not tolerate soggy roots. It is very effective in a rockery. Not only is it to scale for small plants, but it erupts in a mat of bright flowers in the spring.

Have some fun with your mulch. Two shades of aquarium gravel can be arranged in a pattern to suggest a river flowing through, or a mat of moss can serve as a lawn for your fairy garden. Mulching your small hostas not only retains moisture and improves soil texture, it is also a way to set them off.

Growing smaller hostas in the garden

Most little hostas grow best in a dedicated bed or special area set aside in the garden. If combined with larger hostas, they can quickly succumb to root competition, or be overwhelmed by more assertive plants or deprived of water and light by an overhanging leaf—an effective umbrella.

If you do wish to grow your little hostas in a garden, raising the level of the bed is recommended. This accomplishes several things: it enables the gardener to prepare the soil

A miniature hosta contrasting beautifully against a gray rock, a dark green moss, and finely shredded wood mulch.

optimally for the plants; it's easier to weed and care for; it will provide a better opportunity for good drainage; and it brings these diminutive plants closer to the eye so you can enjoy their many charms.

Again, little hostas on the larger end of the scale will do well in standard garden conditions so long as care is taken that they are not overwhelmed by larger plants. Most of the Tiara Series (see chapter six) are vigorous enough for garden planting, provided slugs and snails are kept at bay. A gardener can also improve garden growing conditions by tilling in compost, pine bark fines, well-rotted manure, cocoa shells, or other organic matter to improve soil texture, tilth, and drainage, but these upper-range small plants will grow even without the attention required by the very small and mini varieties.

The smallest hostas can also be planted in the garden, but most will require careful siting, specialized soil preparation, and a sharp eye to note a hosta that is not thriving. If you do notice problems, dig up the affected plant immediately and coddle it in a container until it recovers.

Tips for garden success

• Vary the levels of the bed with rocks, using them as "bumpers" to create small raised areas or tiers. This technique is especially useful on a slope.

Small hostas on a gentle slope arranged into tiers using small rock slabs.

• Separate the small hostas from the rest of the garden, and define them, with flat rocks placed upright and at a slight angle. The angle of the rock will perform an added service by directing rainwater toward the roots of your plants.

• Protect your hostas from snacking slugs and snails by using a mulch of sharp gravel to discourage them. The same gravel worked into the soil and planting holes may deter marauding voles as well. Damage to leaves or roots will more seriously affect the health of a little plant than a similar attack on a bigger hosta. On the reverse side, these hostas are not much of a mouthful for deer and are usually overlooked by that scourge.

Discouraging tree roots

Because hostas do require some shade, they are often planted near or even under trees. But trees are opportunists: when they sense loose, fertile, well-watered soil, their roots naturally

An effective way to plant small hostas is to set them apart with upright stones, which helps both to showcase them and to direct water to their tiny roots.

reach for that "Promised Land." This is not the best news for your hostas. When planting your little hostas out in the garden, you will need to provide them with some protection from root invasion.

Many people are aware that copper deters tree roots. Nurserymen have used this to their advantage for years by employing a fabric coated on one side with a copper preparation. When formed into a pot with the treated surface inside, this fabric keeps the roots from breeching and also from circling inside. Some gardeners have used the aversion of tree roots to copper by turning the fabric pot copper-side-out to discourage tree and other external roots from entering the area where your hostas are planted. A fabric painted with copper on one side can be used as a base for a raised garden—again, with the copper side down. Since most hosta gardens are planted in shady areas where root penetration is a real concern, the fabric should eliminate or at least reduce the problem.

A technique we have used to plant under trees without encouraging root competition or unfairly compromising the tree is to dig out the area in which we intend to grow the hostas to about 15 inches and clear the small roots. We then lay down a triple layer of wet newspaper (weed prevention fabric is also effective but more expensive). On top of that, we spread a 6-inch layer of gravel, and then backfill the area with a good mixture of soil, compost, and pine bark fines. The newspaper and gravel layer will discourage tree root invasion and promote drainage for your hostas.

We have also seen hostas planted in nursery pots and the pots sunk into the garden as a root deterrent. If using this plan, care should be taken that the hostas do not become waterlogged in the pot. This is accomplished by making sure that the planting medium surrounding the pots is more or less the same as that in the containers themselves. We also find that unless the top rim of the container is removed or disguised with mulch, it will detract and distract from your display's appearance. There is one other consideration: you may soon find your carefully placed pot crushed by the surrounding expanding tree roots!

A very clever idea used by hosta growers Bob and Nancy Solberg is the "pot within a pot" scenario. It works like this: a garden is prepared in an area where tree roots are known to invade. Incorporated into the garden are a number of artfully placed, strong-walled pots, sunk into the garden. Potted hostas may then be dropped into these pots and mulch arranged to hide the deception. There are many reasons this is exceedingly clever: the arrangement of the hostas can be changed when the spirit moves you, the interior pots can be removed and tree roots cleared periodically, the potted hostas can be refreshed effortlessly, voles will be discouraged—the list goes on. You may combine some of the earlier scenarios here and add copper-clad fabric to the outside of the outer pot as extra insurance against invasion. We're going to try this idea ourselves.

Growing in raised beds

Little hostas are very content in a raised bed. Building such a bed enables the gardener to create a perfect environment for the plants, while also bringing them to an elevated level where you can appreciate these garden gems and care for them better.

One of the best raised beds we've seen was at the back door of a home where the angle of the house and back steps formed an area ideal for a tall raised bed. This garden was just about waist high; it contained several large rocks (rocks can provide shelter for more delicate hostas and can also act as a latent radiator, absorbing and retaining solar heat), as well as dwarf trees and some interesting mosses. The container itself was built from landscaping timbers. In order for the bed to drain properly, we were told there was a base of stone about a foot deep. On top of the stone was a mixture of volcanic rock, ground pine bark, and garden soil. The rock and ground bark lighten the soil and allow for good drainage. On top was gravel mulch.

This garden has many things to recommend it. The height allows for close viewing of the plants and ease in weeding. The soil mixture is a good one for growing these hostas, and the gravel mulch retains moisture and prevents the small plants from becoming soiled during a heavy rain. And finally, the garden hides an otherwise awkward area.

A hosta rockery

Another quite pleasing variation on the raised bed theme is a rockery for hostas. Some *Hosta* species have adapted to growing in crevices in a rock face in the wild, some developing few leaves to weigh down the plant. That may be extreme for the home gardener, but the point is that smaller hostas are suited to life in a

A very high raised bed built of landscaping timbers brings small plants closer to the eye.

rockery. And while many rock gardens might have a shady side that would be suitable for a few little hostas, it is not difficult to build one especially for hostas.

To build a simple rockery yourself, find a spot where the hostas will receive adequate sun (two or three hours of morning sun is especially desirable). The best way to proceed is to build in layers. Lay the foundation rocks first, add a sharp-draining fill, and then more rocks, with a more hospitable planting mix, continuing this way until your bed is the height and form that you find most pleasing. We recommend planting your hostas as the second-to-last step, taking care to make sure the roots are spread, and including other small plants with similar sun and water requirements (see chapter five). The final step: spread fine gravel mulch, and perhaps paint some of your rocks with yogurt or buttermilk to attract moss, and you have a marvelous place to display your collection.

Siting and sun tolerance

Your little hostas will respond to careful siting. When building a new bed, it is worthwhile to find a spot in your garden where the plants will receive a few hours of morning sunlight and then enjoy a bright but shaded afternoon to relax. Dappled shade is probably optimal for all hosta cultivation, but the ratio of sun to shade becomes even more critical when a plant has a small leaf surface. Some little hostas—for example, those with more white areas—will

Stage 1, constructing a shade garden rockery. The area is outlined with large rocks and backfilled with a planting medium containing about 50 percent gravel.

Stage 2. A second layer of small rocks is arranged on top. Some small hostas are planted in cavities created around the edges.

Stage 3. A final layer of rocks is added, again backfilled, and a fine gravel mulch completes the setting. The result is a free-draining home for a collection of small hostas and miniature companion plants.

need more light to grow but can also be easily damaged by too much sun.

Very broadly speaking, the yellow-leafed hostas (*H.* 'Coconut Custard', *H.* 'Gold Drop', *H.* 'Little Miss Magic', *H.* 'Little Aurora') have greater sun-tolerance, while blue-leafed hostas (*H.* 'Blue Ice', *H.* 'Blue Sliver') are best in shadier areas. Hostas that receive more sun will grow less tall and more tightly. Hostas that receive more shade will grow taller and will spread.

If you have the luxury of choosing a spot where your little ones will be planted, take care to note the garden orientation and how the sun will play across it. If the area you must use is too sunny, you might artfully plant a shrub or ornamental grass to break the harsher rays of the late afternoon. If the chosen area is on a surface such as a patio or deck where planting shade is not an option, the same effect can be achieved with a latticework screen or even a decorative arch.

One of the great advantages to having hostas in pots is that they are portable! If the original place you've chosen to display your collection is not suitable, simple relocate.

Carefully sited in dappled shade, this bed defined by small rocks is an ideal spot for small hostas.

Watering and drainage

Hostas, especially in their first years after planting, need to be watered every other day (depending on weather conditions and soil type), but they cannot tolerate "wet feet." Probably the most important aspect of growing the smallest hostas is ensuring they are adequately watered, yet never wet. As we travel around gardens and interview gardeners looking for "best practice," the common theme is regard for drainage for smaller hostas, most especially the minis. This can be accomplished in various ways. One easy way is to choose a potting mix designed for alpines, which will be grittier. Care should be taken to avoid alkaline mixtures when possible since, again, most hostas will grow better in a slightly acidic or ericaceous soil.

As more of us turn our attention to our outdoor living space and consider how a garden may arouse the senses with textures and aromas in addition to being visually appealing, the soothing notes of a water garden are often included. Little hostas are very much at home along the water, draping gracefully over the edge or being reflected in a quiet pool, but

Hosta 'Blue Ice' beside an artificial stream that creates both sound and movement.

it must be remembered that hostas are not water plants, especially the smaller varieties. We do not recommend planting directly in an earthen pond edge or sinking pots in the water. But they will be stunning massed at the edge in an area raised with rocks or slate, or edging a stream.

Fertilizing

A well-built soil is probably all your hostas require to grow. Some hosta growers never fertilize their plants and judge that the small plants actually do better without artificial feeding. Others claim that regular fertilizing will vastly improve the appearance of your plants.

Chemical fertilizers are of two kinds, balanced and slow-release. The three numbers (12-12-12 or 20-20-20) found on bags of balanced fertilizers refer to an analysis of their relative percentage by weight of nitrogen, phosphorus, and potassium, in that order. The three nutrients promote vegetative growth (nitrogen), root growth (phosphorus), and disease resistance (potassium). All three elements are important for plant growth, and hostas, as flowering foliage plants, are no exception. A feeding in early spring just as the leaves emerge is important, but a second application in early summer (or four to six weeks later) will promote good bloom and also set up your plants to tolerate the winter months to come.

Slow-release fertilizers (sold under brand names like Osmocote or Nutricote) are coated pellets, designed to work in conjunction with soil and air temperature as well as moisture to release fertilizer over time. Your plants, rather than "binge eating," are fertilized gradually for weeks and even months, with less wasted product. The upfront cost is often higher, but the value may be greater.

Organic fertilizers, like herbal remedies for people, are a good source of nutrition, but can be variable in the delivery. The most obvious organic fertilizer is manure. Manure can be purchased composted, dried, and bagged, but it seems silly when most farms and stables are only too happy to have you haul your own. Cow manure is especially plentiful but is often rich in weed seeds. Horse manure from a stable is preferable since horses are often bedded in sawdust, which contains fewer nasty country weed seeds. All manures, especially chicken manure, must be aged and composted thoroughly in order to prevent burning of your plants. The advantage of using manures is that they are more complex than chemical fertilizers, containing micronutrients and trace elements and are released more slowly.

Alfalfa has been grown as a cover crop on farms for hundreds of years. A home gardener can reap the same benefits of the plant by purchasing a 50-pound bag of alfalfa pellets or meal (horse feed, not rabbit feed, which may contain fillers) and either tilling it into the garden or making a "tea" of steeped alfalfa with which to water your hostas.

Crab meal is a byproduct of crab harvesting and is composed of dried and crushed shells as well as some other "remainders." This is primarily a soil conditioner, but it also contains chitin, a substance that may help control foliar nematodes.

Noted hosta grower Warren I. Pollock, of Delaware, has shared his recipes for hosta tonics. Warren has an extensive collection of little hostas, almost all of them containerized, and claims that his tonic regimen promotes stronger and more vigorous growth.

WIP Tonic #1

1 tablespoon liquid seaweed (kelp)
    concentrate
5 drops HB-101 (a plant stimulant containing
    trace elements)
5 drops Superthrive (a growth enhancer
    product)
3 drops wetting agent (mild dish detergent)
1 gallon water

Wet foliage and water into soil about every
other week from early spring through
midsummer.

WIP Tonic #2

1 tablespoon Spray-N-Grow (a foliar-feeding
    micronutrient complex)
3 drops wetting agent (mild dish detergent)
1 gallon warm water

Wet foliage on weeks alternate to WIP Tonic
#1 applications, from early spring through
summer.

The tonics are in addition to fertilizer, not
instead of. It should be noted that any foliar
spray on blue leaves will mark them.

Dividing

Little hostas, as a rule, don't need to be divided.
The obvious reasons for doing so are to keep
a plant in bounds, especially if planted in a
small area or container or the plant is especially vigorous; to correct "male pattern bald-
ness" (a hosta that becomes so crowded that
the center of the crown dies out); or to share
a special plant with a friend. Your little hostas
should not be divided with the same abandon
as you would a large hosta.

When to divide? Little hostas recover best
if left unmolested until after bloom. Shortly
after bloom is completed, your plant will begin
to put out a second flush of growth and make
new roots. Dividing your plant at this time will
enable it to overcome the stress of division and
settle in before dormancy overtakes it in the
winter. The second best time to divide your
little hostas is early in the spring, when they
are first stirring after winter dormancy. Watch
for the signs of buds swelling to tell you this
is occurring, and make sure there is enough
hosta to safely divide.

Do not divide your hosta down to single or
double eyes or buds. You will have the best
results if you ensure each division has five to
six or more eyes.

Hostas can be broken into two general types
when dividing: those that are rhizomatous, and
those that arise from a solid crown. Rhizomatous hostas can be divided by gently pulling
the plant apart. Hostas with eyes arising from
a solid crown must be cut apart using a razor
or boning knife. In both cases, wash the soil
from the roots so that you can see what you're
doing. Make your cut (or determine where to
pull), and then treat any cut area with a 10 percent bleach solution or rooting hormone (most
contain a disinfectant) to discourage bacteria.
Care should be taken to damage as few roots
as possible. Your tools as well should be kept
clean and bacteria-free by rinsing in a 10 percent bleach solution between plants.

Winter care

Hostas are herbaceous perennials that do best
in areas that experience at least forty days of
frost. Although they can be grown in warmer
climates, most hostas will not perform as well
as they do in areas with colder winters.

In the coldest areas, hostas are given a pro-
tective winter mulch in order to keep the

temperature more constant and, therefore, avoid the possibility of heaving (a condition where the repeated freezing and thawing of the soil forces a plant up and out of the ground, exposing the crown and tender roots to freezing temperatures and drying winds). In milder climates, mulching to prevent frost heave may not be necessary. Newly planted hostas, especially, can suffer from heaving during cold winter months if not protected by a layer of mulch.

We live in the western New York area very close to the Canadian border. We receive about 100 inches of snow each winter, and our temperatures can fall well below freezing for days at a time. We have wintered our hostas in pots both inside (in an unheated garage) and outside, and we find that they will do best if left outside, with precautions, provided that the container is frost-proof.

The problem with an unprotected container is that a cold day will cause the soil to freeze, and then a sunny day may thaw only the top layer. Water can then pool and, with no opportunity to drain through the frozen potting mix below, cause the dormant plant to rot. The solution is, therefore, maintaining constant soil temperatures, making sure that your potted hostas are in containers that will not break up in winter conditions and providing some protection against critter damage (voles, mice, etc).

The most effective arrangement we have found is to collect the hostas into a sheltered

A wooden corral containing potted hostas covered with a shredded wood mulch for winter protection.

area—somewhere where they will not receive direct sun and they are out of drying winds. If you don't have such a place naturally, you can build a "corral"—a wooden frame with small gauge chicken wire or hardware cloth on the bottom to discourage rodent invasion. We place all our pots in a rectangular corral so that they are as close together as possible and in contact with the ground. We fill any gaps with shredded cedar mulch (which allows drainage and some air circulation and is not a favorite of voles). As added insurance, we add some rodent bait—the waxed type that can withstand weather. We do this well before the snow or severe weather, usually late November, but you can adjust earlier or later depending on your season. Once the foliage has fully died back, we cover the entire area with 4 to 6 inches of mulch. We then ignore it until spring, when we will begin removing the top layer of mulch little by little.

Hostas that are in the ground will probably do just fine, but a layer of mulch would be added insurance. Voles are voracious, and so some effort should be expended to discourage them from dining on your crowns—either rodent bait, or chicken wire pinned over the sleeping plants.

Some very early emerging hostas, like *H*. 'Roller Coaster Ride', stand the risk of being damaged by a late frost, so be prepared with newspapers, flowerpots, tarps, or discarded lampshades if tender shoots have emerged and a frost is predicted.

The winter care for plants in milder climates is slightly different. Potted hostas may be moved into a sheltered area, such as under the eaves of a house or into an unheated garage. Take care to provide water if nature does not, so that the crowns do not totally dry out. You may need to artificially water once or twice during the season.

Having said all this about protecting your plants, over the years we have missed the odd hosta which was left to fend for itself in a corner of the garden, and in most cases, it did just fine. We don't recommend just leaving them, but if you miss one, chances are, you'll probably get away with it.

When bad things happen to good hostas

Hostas are relatively problem-free plants, but they do have some challenges with creatures and diseases, as we've already hinted. Here's a bit more about the most important of these.

Deer love hostas but will probably ignore your smallest plants in favor of something more suited to a deer-sized appetite. Voles, however, can be a serious problem. A vole is a rodent resembling a mouse (and is sometimes even called a field mouse). Voles make shallow tunnels and are voracious eaters of plant material, especially tasty hosta crowns. There is nothing more discouraging than having the snow melt in the spring and finding a tunnel and a label where your favorite hosta once stood.

If you have a vole problem, you can be proactive in preventing damage by either planting your garden hostas in a wire basket or mixing sharp gravel into the planting hole. A determined vole may breech these defenses, but most will look for easier targets.

The choice of control depends on the magnitude of your vole population and your personal tolerance for quelling the damage. If you don't mind sending the offending creatures to heaven, there are waxed baits that can be strategically placed where you know voles to be active. It is recommended that the baits be placed inside flexible tubing and the tubing placed in the vole run and secured with wire, to prevent other animals from ingesting the bait. Another strategy is to place the bait under a weighted pot. Remember that if the deceased vole becomes the dinner of something a bit higher up the food chain, they too could be affected.

You may live-trap your voles—but then what? Who receives your pest? There are also mouse traps that may be baited with peanut butter and placed under an upturned flower pot.

Slugs and snails

Slugs and snails are a constant problem for hosta growers. Something about the succulent leaves of a hosta will bring in the gastropods and wreak havoc on your plants. Again, control is somewhat dependent upon your personal convictions and your tolerance for damage to your plants.

You can deter slugs and snails by mulching with a substance that they would prefer not to crawl upon. Diatomaceous earth is the fossilized remains of a type of algae, and it is accepted that slugs and snails will avoid crawling over it. A ring around your plants may be all you need. Coffee grounds have also been said to adversely affect slugs and snails, and so a ring of grounds around your plant may also protect it, while offering some minor benefit to the soil.

If your hosta is potted, setting the pot in a tray of water will keep slugs away since they do not swim. Or placing a rim of copper on the pot will create a weak electrical field that repels the creatures. Spraying a non-porous container with WD-40 will keep them from crawling up the sides.

If you wish to rid your garden of slugs and snails, not just discourage them, you may skulk around in the dark, especially after a rain, with a flashlight and a plastic bag. When your light picks out a slug, scoop it up and deposit it into the bag, which is eventually tied and tossed into the garbage.

A spray of ammonia and water (10 percent ammonia) sprayed directly on a slug will cause it to shrivel while not harming your plant. The bad news is that it will not discourage the next slug, only dispense with the slugs that actually come in contact with the spray.

Everyone knows about beer traps and scattering citrus rinds about the garden to collect slugs, so we won't bore you by repeating those techniques here.

Slug bait is really the best way to deal with a slug problem. Used properly, the bait will not harm other wildlife but will effectively rid your garden of slugs. The correct way to use the bait is to begin early in the spring, before the plants have even emerged, so as to get to the slugs before they lay eggs. The bait is broadcast very sparingly, and the application is repeated every two weeks. If this program is followed without fail, you will gradually rid your garden of current slugs and their children, grandchildren, and great-grandchildren; expect a good result within three years.

Disease

Petiole rot, formerly known as southern blight, is now an equal opportunity scourge. The condition is caused by a soil-borne fungus that will cause the hosta petioles, or leaf stems, to rot at the base. The best control is prevention, and the best prevention is to keep mulch from contact with your plant. Because it is soil-borne, if you do suspect it, do not move the plant, but treat it in place with a 10 percent bleach solution. There are fungicides available as well; consult with staff at your favorite nursery about the correct one to use, and the correct way to use it.

Foliar nematodes are microscopic wormlike creatures that invade the leaves of hostas. Late in the summer, infected plants will show yellowish brown streaks between the leaf veins. Foliar nematodes can spread quickly through watering or growing plants close together. There are various techniques to control foliar nematodes, which are beyond the scope of this book. We recommend choosing plants carefully from reputable growers, watching new plants for the first year, and destroying any plants that turn up with a problem.

Finally, hostas are susceptible to various viruses, but the most visible and serious is Hosta Virus X (HVX). The virus shows up as a mottling of the leaves. At this writing, there is no remedy for the home gardener, and the plant should be immediately discarded (not in your compost heap, please). The best guarantee that your garden will not be affected or infected is to be aware of the virus's appearance (see www.americanhostasociety.org), and purchase symptom-free plants from reputable growers.

Mapping and labeling

Hosta collectors like to keep track of the varieties they grow. Mapping troughs, gardens, and pots is not difficult. By mapping your garden,

you avoid the "mouse graveyard" look of too many labels, and you can identify a plant if you need to. When preparing the map, it is important to link the map to the area with either a garden name (peach tree garden, second-tier garden), a landmark ("left of the mossy rock"), or some system of numbers. For heaven's sake, orient the map when you do so, please. The key is making it easy to find a hosta's name when you want to. We still remember with amusement a dear friend who insisted on only mapping his garden. But he could never remember the orientation of his maps, so he would page through his garden map book and then begin spinning in place until he was satisfied he was pointed in the right direction.

The downside of having a map and no label is that a visitor will not be able to identify a plant without asking and having you rush off to find your information. If, however, you want to keep track of your hostas' names and also enable visitors to easily see what's what, even if you are not available, the best thing to do is label. Often a label comes with your plant, but it can be garish or out of scale, especially with mini hostas, and will disrupt the mood you are trying to establish. You may also find that a clutter of labels of any size detracts from your planting, but you still want to be able to identify a plant easily.

For the serious hosta gardener, we recommend three labels: one next to the plant, one under the hosta in the planting hole, and one saved in a file on the computer or garden book with a reference to the site. If this seems like overkill, you'll think differently when a bird or squirrel carries off your label and you are left with an orphan plant.

There are many, many label styles, materials,

and techniques available. Choose the one that works best in your garden.

Ideas for labels

• Paint pen on smooth stone. Paint pens can be purchased in hobby shops. Choose a dark color if you will be using light-colored stones and a light color if you will be using black stones. The name can either be written on the top of the stone and placed near the plant, or can become part of the landscape by turning the stone over. The same technique may be used on pieces of slate or terracotta.

• Etched metal. There are plant labels available made of soft copper or aluminum with a stylus provided. The name is imprinted into the soft metal and will never fade. Some are attractive enough to display with your plant; some are utilitarian and may be pushed into the soil nearby.

• Permanent marker on white plastic. One of the least ideal type of plant label for several reasons. A "permanent marker" is never permanent. Trust us on this! Sun, rain, and time have a way of rendering your label unreadable. The exception is No. 2 pencil (soft), which will probably last longer than your plastic label. Plastic also becomes brittle in the weather, and one spring morning you may find only a shard left. Another trick to improve longevity of both plastic

Hosta names written on stones and bits of broken pottery can be placed next to small hostas and turned over, so as not to detract from the beauty of the plant.

label and permanent marker is to invert the label and push it into the ground so that only the pointed tip is showing. The label can be pulled to read the name if necessary, and the soil will protect writing and plastic longer than leaving it exposed to weather.

• Wooden sticks. Less obtrusive than white plastic but will deteriorate even faster. Not recommended unless you intend on replacing labels frequently and you have a good map.

• Metal manufactured labels. There are zinc, copper, and stainless steel plant markers available from many sources that are to scale and will last for many years. Try to avoid the type where the sides of the label face wrap around the stake; we have found this type of label becomes easily separated from the label stake. We prefer the style where the label posts fit through the label face. You can use a paint pen to write on the face or a No. 2 pencil.

• "Label maker" machines. Various ones are in commerce. One type punches raised letters onto a plastic, adhesive strip. It's an inexpensive way to label but will soon lose its charm if you have more than a few labels to do at one sitting, or if you are labeling your *H.* 'Silver Threads and Golden Needles'. A label maker that we use has a keyboard and

A white plastic label pushed into the ground with only the tip showing to both make it less obtrusive and protect the "permanent" marking.

special laminated tape. You are able to type out your hosta's name, print out the tape, and then affix it to the label of your choice. The machines have become less expensive than in the past, but the tape is still not cheap. The attraction is that this label will last indefinitely and retains its legibility and good looks. We think black letters on clear tape or white letters on black tape look best. We have also used this laminated tape on black plastic signs to good effect.

You may come up with an ingenious homemade method of labeling your hostas not mentioned here. We have seen labels laboriously cut from beer cans, labels made from mini blinds liberated on trash day, labels made from any number of found objects. However you decide to keep track of your hostas, it needs to be relatively simple or you won't do it, and it should also look good with your collection.

Record keeping

If, over time, you find yourself becoming even more keenly interested in your plants, you may wish to keep records. The simplest record, of course, is the one just mentioned—a list of your plants and where they are planted. But there are other records to keep.

• Where and when you purchased your hosta

• Who hybridized your hosta and what year it was introduced into commerce; many catalogs will have this information, but the best resource is the American Hosta Society's Hosta Registry and/or Hosta Library (see "Further Reading")

• Fertilizing history and results

• Observations on the plant's habit

• Flowering style, time, and fragrance

• Fertility

You may even wish to try hybridizing one day—that is, transferring pollen from the stamen of one plant onto the pistil of the other. You will appreciate your progress best if you have kept track of which pollen you used and which plant set the pod.

Your records can be as detailed or as casual as you want them to be, but keeping records, in some fashion, does add yet another dimension to your hobby. And a final note: keeping the most basic record, a list of your plants, *might* keep you from unintentionally purchasing a hosta already in your garden.

A mature raised bed, behind a moss-covered stone wall, with miniature plants tucked into crevices and with levels created with additional rock work to add interest.

CHAPTER FOUR

Creating a Place for Little Hostas

ONE OF THE GREAT JOYS of growing little hostas is finding new and creative places to display them. Large hostas are garden plants (there is a limit as to the size of container one can move!), but small hostas adapt well to an enormous range of planting sites, enabling the resourceful gardener to "think outside the garden." A substantial collection of plants will grow happily even for those living in apartments and condominiums. A full hosta garden can even be planted in the window box, and an arrangement of three hostas in a terracotta bowl, with an interesting rock for contrast, makes an elegant centerpiece on an outdoor table.

Gardens reflect the needs, lifestyle, and personality of the gardener. A person's garden is an artistic expression, no matter how it is presented. Some people prefer a very formal look, with straight lines and rows of plants, almost like a crop; some prefer to create garden "rooms" that must be entered to be enjoyed; some tend toward the happy jumble of a cottage garden. A place can be created for little hostas in all types of garden designs. The garden you plan should be the one that meets your personal needs and preference. Our objective is not to tell you how to plan your garden, but rather what styles might work best

with the smaller hostas and how to get the best from the design you use.

The miniature, very small, and small hostas do not always appreciate the wide-open spaces of the large garden or yard. They will do better in their own environment, separated from larger plants. Make sure your little hosta garden is in an area where it can be appreciated and where it can be easily maintained. It is our experience that the little hostas are best off closer to the house, perhaps near a front door or along a walkway. It makes sense from a care point of view and also from a stylistic standpoint: small plants might look forlorn in a faraway island.

Giving your little hostas their own space can be as simple as mounding the soil in a selected area of the garden, with the soil deepest at the center, or setting aside an area of your garden with upright slate slabs, timbers, or rock. You will want to call attention to the site you have selected, so that your little hostas shine. Because they are smaller, there is real value to raising the bed when possible for maximum effect. The most obvious advantage of a raised bed is that it will bring small plants closer to the eye, so that they may be appreciated fully; an additional advantage is that a raised bed will naturally enjoy good drainage. A raised bed might be a built structure near your back door or patio, or it can be a section of garden that is raised with timbers, rocks, or edging.

We like the look of different levels, rather than of a flat expanse, when growing little plants. Levels add to the interest and, like artwork on a dais, help the plants to show off. Levels can be created with stone (a sinuous line of stone holding up a tier), with lawn edging, or with mounded soil. You can plant your dedicated space with hostas alone or create a landscape in miniature; many small shrubs, trees, conifers, and perennials will carry out the small or miniature theme (see chapter five).

The most important element to successful growing of the smaller hostas is soil structure and composition. Because these plants tend to have more delicate roots that are closer to the surface of the soil, the texture should be more loose and friendly to those roots. We recommend taking the time to amend your soil liberally with organic matter and some kind of particulate (see the list on page 29 for examples) or even small coarse gravel, so that the result is an airy loose soil, rich in humus and unlikely to allow water to pool. Please see the previous chapter for more detail on building good soil at the start.

Ranks of small contrasting hostas growing well in a simple raised bed along the side of a house.

A miniature hosta almost hidden under a very large *H.* 'Earth Angel', where it will probably be deprived of both light and water.

A single line of bricks defines a bed for little hostas, but this arrangement does not bring them closer to the eye.

A collection of hostas in a raised bed separated from other plants with rocks and stones.

A raised bed in dappled shade provides an ideal setting for small hostas.

The ideal garden site will receive two or three hours of morning sun and then be in the shade the rest of the day. Try to avoid the opposite scenario, having sun at the end of the day. When planting directly into your garden bed, you will need to be attentive to the eventual size of your hostas, so that the very small are not overwhelmed by the more robust. We've seen more than one little hosta deprived of rain under the umbrella-like leaf of a much larger hosta nearby. On the other hand, hostas are very portable and forgiving plants, and if your tableau is becoming unbalanced, scoop up a hosta or two and reset them.

Although there are hostas that can fend for themselves along with larger plants, we believe you are doing little hostas a disservice if they are not given at least a few dedicated square feet to call their own.

Hostas suitable for raised beds

Hosta 'Baby Bunting'

LEAVES. Heart-shaped, almost round, blue-green early in season, turning mid-green later, 2½ × 2 in. (6 × 5 cm)

CLUMP. Densely packed, compact, 10 × 20 in. (25 × 50 cm)

In a shady spot, this easy-to-grow cultivar quickly forms a dense mound. Ideal for the raised bed and the woodland garden or walk.

Hosta 'Blue Sliver'

LEAVES. Narrow, very pointed and slightly wavy, blue-green, 7 × 2 in. (18 × 5 cm)

CLUMP. Flat and irregular, 8 × 18 in. (20 × 45 cm)

Very tolerant of shade and ideal for the woodland garden and the raised bed.

Hosta 'Blueberry Tart'

LEAVES. Oval, folded and slightly wavy, mid-blue, 4½ × 2½ in. (11 × 6 cm)

CLUMP. Fairly fast-growing and tight, 8 × 18 in. (20 × 45 cm)

In dappled shade will maintain color through the season. Good for the raised bed and woodland garden.

Hosta 'Calypso'

LEAVES. Long and narrow, folded to the midrib, pale yellow, quickly turning white, with a dark green margin, 6½ × 2½ in. (17 × 6 cm)
CLUMP. A neat, tall rosette, 10 × 16 in. (25 × 40 cm)

One of the fastest growing and easiest of the medio-variegated varieties. Provides a good color contrast in raised beds, woodland walks, and large containers.

Hosta 'Candy Cane'

LEAVES. Tapering and slightly rippled, mid-green with an irregular cream margin, 6 × 2½ in. (15 × 6 cm)

CLUMP. Fairly dense, fast-growing, arching, 8 × 12 in. (20 × 30 cm)

Grows well in morning sun or dappled shade. Ideal for the woodland walk, large container, and raised beds.

Hosta 'Cheatin Heart'

LEAVES. Oval to heart-shaped, slightly wavy, chartreuse aging to dull gold, 3½ × 3 in. (9 × 8 cm)

CLUMP. Compact and dense, 7 × 15 in. (18 × 38 cm)

Given more sun, the color becomes an even more intense orange-gold. Looks good in the trough or tray and will do well in even the larger raised bed and woodland garden once mature.

Hosta 'Dew Drop'

LEAVES. Almost round, dark green with a narrow white margin, 3 × 2½ in. (8 × 6 cm)

CLUMP. Flattish, 7 × 12 in. (18 × 30 cm)

Grows best in dappled shade; too much sun can cause a "drawstring" effect. Excellent for the woodland garden and raised bed.

Hosta 'Green with Envy'

LEAVES. Oval to nearly round, greenish white to dark yellow with narrow dark green margin, 3 × 2 in. (8 × 5 cm)

CLUMP. Tight with maturity, 10 × 15 in. (25 × 38 cm)

Emerges early in the spring and retains its color throughout the season if kept out of direct sunlight.

Hosta 'Hi Ho Silver'

LEAVES. Lance-shaped, mid-green with a variable bright white margin extending down the petiole, 6 × 2 in. (15 × 5 cm)

CLUMP. Loose and unruly, 8 × 12 in. (20 × 30 cm)

Too much sun will likely damage the thin leaves of this otherwise very attractive cultivar. It looks good against dark mulch in a raised bed or woodland garden. *Hosta* 'Sarah Kennedy' and *H.* 'Ginko Craig' are both very similar.

Hosta 'Holy Mouse Ears'

LEAVES. Almost round, white with a blue-green margin, 2 × 2 in. (5 × 5 cm)

CLUMP. A slow-growing, flat rosette, 6 × 12 in. (15 × 30 cm)

In dappled shade matures slowly into a pretty, flat mound, ideal for the trough or the front of a raised bed.

Hosta 'Island Charm'

LEAVES. Oval, creamy white with a wide green margin, 4 × 3 in. (10 × 8 cm)

CLUMP. Fairly slow-growing, dense and domed, 9 × 15 in. (23 × 38 cm)

Early morning sun can improve the growth rate. Ideal for the woodland garden and raised beds.

Hosta 'Kiwi Blue Baby'

LEAVES. Oval, thick, with good substance, very blue, 5 × 3½ in. (13 × 9 cm)

CLUMP. Slow-growing, neat, and low, 8 × 15 in. (20 × 38 cm)

Prefers dappled to medium shade and looks good planted to the front of a raised bed or in the woodland garden.

Hosta 'Lakeside Baby Face'

LEAVES. Heart-shaped, very shiny dark green with a dark yellow margin, 2 × 2 in. (5 × 5 cm)

CLUMP. Fast-growing, with leaves held apart on strong petioles, 7 × 12 in. (18 × 30 cm)

Grows well in good light—and larger than the registered size, in our experience. Ideal for the woodland walk and larger raised bed.

Hosta 'Lakeside Cupcake'

LEAVES. Rounded, deeply cupped, white with a wide, dark blue-green margin, 4 × 4 in. (10 × 10 cm)

CLUMP. Low and dense, 5 × 15 in. (13 × 38 cm)

In good light quickly forms an impressive mound. A standout hosta in a woodland walk or raised bed.

Hosta 'Little Bo Peep'

LEAVES. Long, tapering, and glossy. Bright green with a wide, irregular white margin, 4 × 1 in. (10 × 3 cm)

CLUMP. Open and arching, 5 × 9 in. (13 × 23 cm)

A striking hosta that also does well in a woodland walk and in a large trough.

Hosta 'Little White Lines'

LEAVES. Oval, slightly rippled, mid-green with a crisp narrow white edge, 4 × 2 in. (10 × 5 cm)

CLUMP. Low and wide, 10 × 30 in. (25 × 75 cm)

Does best in dappled shade and is ideally suited to the wood-land garden and larger raised beds. Similar to *H.* 'Striker', *H.* 'Bunchoko', *H.* 'Allan P. McConnell'.

Hosta 'Minnie Bell'

LEAVES. Oval with a pronounced point and a slight wave, dark green with a pale yellow margin, 3 × 1 in. (8 × 3 cm)

CLUMP. Dense, 8 × 20 in. (20 × 50 cm)

Light to moderate shade will bring out the best in this plant. Striking foliage. Suits the larger raised bed and big container.

Hosta 'OHS Calamari'

LEAVES. Lance-shaped, shiny and wavy, dark green with a creamy white center that extends down the petiole, 7 × 1 in. (18 × 3 cm)

CLUMP. Fairly fast-growing, circular rosette, 7 × 20 in. (18 × 50 cm)

Will enjoy several hours of sun provided it gets plenty of water. An ideal plant for the raised bed and larger containers.

Hosta 'Ops'

LEAVES. Heart-shaped, mid-green with an irregular creamy yellow margin, 3 × 2 in. (8 × 5 cm)

CLUMP. Fairly fast-growing, neat, 6 × 12 in. (15 × 30 cm)

Distinctive foliage and very attractive. Does best in early morning sun and dappled shade. Ideal for the woodland garden and raised bed.

Hosta 'Pixie Vamp'

LEAVES. Heart-shaped to oval, mid-green with a wide, irregular creamy white margin. Some streaking may occur. 2½ × 2 in. (6 × 5 cm)

CLUMP. A perfect low-grower, 6 × 12 in. (15 × 30 cm)

A very pretty hosta that will enhance the front of a raised bed and look good in a large trough. Best kept out of bright sunshine in warmer climates.

Hosta 'Plug Nickel'

LEAVES. Oval, slightly folded and very shiny, bright dark green, 3½ × 2½ in. (9 × 6 cm)

CLUMP. Neat, domed, and very fast-growing. 7 × 15 in. (18 × 38 cm)

Leaves may burn in too much sun. Ideal for the border, raised bed, and large trough.

Hosta 'Popo'

LEAVES. Oval, blue-gray, 2½ × 1½ in. (6 × 4 cm)

CLUMP. Dense and fairly fast-growing, 7 × 18 in. (18 × 45 cm)

Needs some early morning sun in cooler climates, where it will hold its color until late in the season. Will grow well in a woodland garden, raised beds, and larger containers.

Hosta 'Ray of Hope'

LEAVES. Elliptic, heavily rippled and slightly wavy, mid-green with dark yellow streaks that turn light green later in the season, 5 × 2 in. (13 × 5 cm)

CLUMP. Loose, with a moderate growth rate, 6 × 12 in. (15 × 30 cm)

Grows well in dappled shade and will look good in a raised bed or large container.

Hosta 'Soft Shoulders'

LEAVES. Elliptic to oval, slightly undulating and neatly tapering to a sharp point, dark green with a narrow white margin, 8 × 3 in. (20 × 8 cm)

CLUMP. Upright and moderately fast-growing, 10 × 18 in. (25 × 45 cm)

A larger plant that needs space to achieve its potential. Ideal for the back of a larger raised bed and in the woodland garden.

Hosta 'Tick Tock'

LEAVES. Heart-shaped and pointed, folded and sometimes wavy, with good substance, chartreuse-green with a wide green-blue edge, 4 × 2½ in. (10 × 6 cm)

CLUMP. A low, dense rosette, 6 × 10 in. (15 × 25 cm)

Slow-growing but sun-tolerant in cooler climates. The thick leaves are very slug-resistant, and it will do well in a raised bed or woodland garden.

Hosta 'Winsome'

LEAVES. Broadly oval, dark green with a fairly wide, somewhat irregular creamy white margin, 4×3 in. (10×8 cm)

CLUMP. A tight, regular mound, 10 $\times$ 20 in. (25×50 cm)

Prefers to grow in dappled shade and will make a feature plant in a raised bed or woodland garden. *Hosta* 'Thumbelina' is similar but with paler leaves.

Woodland settings

Even in a very small space, the opportunity to grow some of the wide variety of small woodland plants should not be missed. A natural woodland offers so many challenges to the gardener that the creation of an artificial woodland bed or corner is really a better solution. True woodland includes high trees, smaller trees and shrubs, and an understory that depends on the amount of light reaching the ground through the canopy. Too much light, and the ground is often covered in a dense mass of unruly plants such as bramble, vines, and poison ivy. Little or no light usually results in sterile areas beneath the trees, with only fallen leaves and branches to provide interest, and further indicates poor soil shot through with roots. Better to find a shaded place near a building to create your woodland style garden, or build your own.

The varying colors and heights of these small hostas make an interesting show in the woodland garden of Clarence and Betty Owens in Jackson, Michigan.

A mature woodland planting with small hostas *H.* 'First Mate' and *H.* 'Bitsy Gold' in the foreground.

A newly constructed woodland walk on the shady side of a small garden.

Hostas, as shade-tolerant plants, are particularly suited for the woodland garden. You don't need a forest to create the look, but if you can find an out-of-the-way section of the yard that will accept some ornamental trees, you are on your way.

Woodland gardens often have very changeable light patterns. A wooded area of deciduous trees will be bright in the spring and then much shadier as the leaves sprout and elongate. If you are able, assess the area in summer before planning your garden. Limb up taller trees to let in more light if necessary, or if planting from the beginning, look for trees with lacier foliage that will allow enough light for your hostas to thrive.

Roots are another consideration in the woodland garden. Some trees are rooted more deeply than others and will not affect your hostas, but many trees have shallow root systems. Norway maples, for example, are notorious for having shallow roots that will be a constant problem, quickly growing into the root systems of your hostas. Oaks and most nut trees are deep rooted and will be less of a nuisance. Also, in case you've got concerns about walnuts and hostas, they will get along just fine, but you do need to be aware of companions that may not appreciate the juglone produced by walnuts, butternuts, and hickories.

When planting your woodland, take notice of how plants grow in the forest. There are generally three layers of growth: the canopy, the understory, and finally the ground level. The canopy is formed by the trees themselves; the higher the canopy, the better the light below. The understory is comprised of smaller trees, such as dogwood and redbud, and shrubs like rhododendron, buckeye, and oakleaf hydrangea. Finally, we have the woodland floor—a delightful canvas upon which to create the dense, informal style of the forest floor.

A woodland garden, even on a small scale, will look best if the plant height is varied. Select small hostas that display a variety of form—upright, domed, and rhizomatous spreading types. This is not the place for very small or mini hostas, unless you choose from the more assertive cultivars.

The path of a woodland garden is just as important as the plants. A good path showcases and complements the plants along it and defines the vantage point from which the plants are viewed. The smaller the plant, the closer it needs to be to the pathway in order to appreciate its beauty. Plants that, although small, bulk up into slightly larger clumps can be further from the eye and still enjoyed. A small woodland setting with maybe a meandering pathway gives the opportunity to grow a selection of the larger clumps a little further from the walk.

Hosta 'Academy Verdant Verge'

LEAVES. Broadly oval, rippled, mid-green, 3 × 1 in. (8 × 3 cm). **CLUMP.** Hemispherical, congested, 8 × 15 in. (20 × 38 cm).

Extremely vigorous and will grow quickly almost anywhere. Will take a little sun. Multiple dark flowers held on very tall scapes.

Hosta 'Baby Blue Eyes'

LEAVES. Heart-shaped, slightly corrugated, medium blue-green, glaucous above and below, 3½ × 2½ in. (9 × 7 cm) **CLUMP.** Neat, 6 × 12 in. (15 × 30 cm)

The attractive bloom on the leaves will be lost if it is grown in bright sunshine, but in light shade it is a rapid grower and increases quickly.

Hosta 'Bedazzled'

LEAVES. Wedge-shaped, dark green with a wide yellow margin, 5½ × 4½ in. (14 × 11 cm)

CLUMP. Flat and unruly, 8 × 20 in. (20 × 50 cm)

Best in dappled shade. The leaves are large for a small hosta, but the very low growth habit makes it suitable for the front of a raised bed or a woodland garden.

Hosta 'Binkie'

LEAVES. Yellow with a wide, irregular mid-green margin, 4 × 3 in. (10 × 8 cm)

CLUMP. Fairly fast-growing, low and loose, 7 × 14 in. (18 × 35 cm)

A lovely and robust sport of *H.* 'Amber Tiara'. Takes sun in cooler climates and some early morning sun further south. Easy to grow and pest-resistant, it is therefore suitable for the woodland garden.

Hosta 'Bob Olson'

LEAVES. Oval at maturity, dark green with a creamy white, slightly rippled margin, 3½ × 2 in. (9 × 5 cm)

CLUMP. Upright, 6 × 12 in. (15 × 30 cm)

Grows fast and well in a sunny spot. Emerges early in spring before the woodland trees are in full leaf.

Hosta 'Cracker Crumbs'

LEAVES. Broadly oval, shiny bright yellow, turning to chartreuse as the season progresses, with a dark green margin, 2½ × 1½ in. (6 × 4 cm)

CLUMP. Solid, with a moderate growth rate, 6 × 12 in. (15 × 30 cm)

Enjoys morning sun and then dappled shade. Looks lovely in the woodland garden with early emerging spring companion plants. Also good in a raised bed, where it will stand out against dark mulch.

Hosta 'Dixie Chick'

LEAVES. Broadly lance-shaped to oval, slightly wavy, shiny dark green with a narrow white margin that sometimes shows green flecks, 3 × 2 in. (8 × 5 cm)
CLUMP. Fast-growing, flattish, 6 × 15 in. (15 × 38 cm)

Will grow well in early morning sun. Ideal for the woodland walk and an excellent plant for the trough and raised bed.

Hosta 'Fireworks'

LEAVES. Spindle-shaped and slightly twisted, white with a mid-green margin and some streaking, 5 × 1½ in. (13 × 4 cm)

CLUMP. Unruly but moderately fast-growing, 7 × 15 in. (18 × 38 cm)

Cannot take much sun in warmer climates and prefers dappled shade. Ideal as a contrast in collections of small hostas with plainer foliage.

Hosta 'Grand Prize'

LEAVES. Heart-shaped, mid-green with a wide bright yellow margin, 4½ × 3½ in. (11 × 9 cm)

CLUMP. Tall and loose, 9 × 15 in. (23 × 38 cm)

An outstanding small hosta.

Dappled shade will maintain the excellent color contrast. A sport of *H*. 'Grand Tiara'.

Hosta 'Hacksaw'

LEAVES. Long, tapering, narrow, heavily rippled, slightly serrated, light green, 8 × 1 in. (20 × 3 cm)

CLUMP. Flat and loose, 8 × 12 in. (20 × 30 cm)

Good sun tolerance ensures a vigorous growth rate and a bright color, although it may grow bigger than expected.

Hosta 'Hidden Cove'

LEAVES. Narrow and pointed with a slight twist, chartreuse to light green with a darker green margin, 5 × 2 in. (13 × 5 cm)

CLUMP. A tight mound of distinctive foliage, 6 × 12 in. (15 × 30 cm)

In optimum conditions of good light and plenty of water, it can grow larger than expected, so best placed at the back of a raised bed or in a woodland garden.

Hosta 'Lakeside Dragonfly'

LEAVES. Broadly lance-shaped, tapering to a fine point and arching downward, medium blue-green with a white margin, 7 × 3 in. (18 × 8 cm)

CLUMP. Fast-growing and tall, 12 × 26 in. (30 × 65 cm)

In good light and a well-drained soil, this variety may approach medium size, but its fast growth rate and striking foliage make it ideal for the woodland walk and the back of a raised bed. It will also look good by itself in a ceramic pot.

Hosta 'Lakeside Miss Muffett'

LEAVES. Oval, pointed, slightly rippled, mid-green with a wide white border, 4 × 3 in. (10 × 8 cm)

CLUMP. Fast-growing, neat, upward-facing rosette, 6 × 18 in. (15 × 45 cm)

Grows well in many lightly shaded situations. Ideal for the large container, raised bed, and woodland walk.

Hosta 'Lakeside Prissy Miss'

LEAVES. Oval, pointed, and very wavy, bright yellow with a narrow white margin, 7 × 4 in. (18 × 10 cm)

CLUMP. Tight, fast-growing, 9 × 18 in. (23 × 45 cm)

Will take some sunshine in cooler climates and is an ideal plant for the woodland garden and woodland walk.

Hosta 'Lily Blue Eyes'

LEAVES. Oval, lightly wavy with a serrated edge, blue-green, white-backed, 8 × 5 in. (20 × 13 cm)
CLUMP. Dense but untidy, 10 × 20 in. (25 × 50 cm)

The glaucous bloom is lost in direct sunlight, so an ideal hosta for the woodland garden.

Hosta 'Little Aurora'

LEAVES. Cupped and slightly rugose, bright yellow, 4 × 3 in. (10 × 8 cm)

CLUMP. Fairly flat and tight, 10 × 20 in. (25 × 50 cm)

Needs early morning sun to bring out good color. An ideal plant to provide color contrast in a mixed planting.

Hosta 'Little Miss Magic'

LEAVES. Lance-shaped, pointed, slightly rippled and moderately wavy, bright yellow in spring, light green later, 7 × 2 in. (18 × 5 cm)

CLUMP. Moderately cascading habit, 8 × 18 in. (20 × 45 cm)

Emerges early in the spring and will take some sun, eventually forming a lovely loose mound.

Hosta 'Little Wonder'

LEAVES. Oval, dark green with a creamy white margin, 2½ × 1½ in. (6 × 4 cm)

CLUMP. Very tight, dome-shaped, 7 × 12 in. (18 × 30 cm)

Grows well in good light. The regular shape makes it ideal for containers and troughs when small and for raised beds and shady gardens when mature. Similar to *H.* 'Winsome' and *H.* 'Thumbelina'.

Hosta 'Paradise Puppet'

LEAVES. Elongated teardrop, slightly folded, mid-green, 2½ × 1½ in. (6 × 4 cm)

CLUMP. Low, fast-spreading but loose, 6 × 20 in. (15 × 50 cm)

An ideal small groundcover plant that can mature into a very wide and irregular low mound. Can be used effectively to fill spaces between more upright and colorful cultivars.

Hosta 'Rhythm and Blues'

LEAVES. Long, narrow, very wavy, blue turning green later in the season, 6 × 2½ in. (15 × 6 cm)

CLUMP. Fast-growing and tall, 10 × 24 in. (25 × 60 cm)

Needs to be kept cool and out of the bright sun in warmer climates. This distinctive plant is ideal for the raised bed and woodland garden, where it will multiply rapidly.

Hosta 'Roller Coaster Ride'

LEAVES. Lance-shaped, heavily rippled and shiny dark green with a narrow yellow-white margin, 6 × 2 in. (15 × 5 cm)

CLUMP. Busy yet loose, arching, 10 × 18 in. (25 × 45 cm)

Emerges very early in spring and might require protection from late frosts. Fast-growing and large enough for a woodland walk or raised bed.

Hosta 'Shiro Kabitan'

LEAVES. Ribbonlike with a slight twist, white with a narrow green margin, 4½ × 1½ in. (11 × 4 cm)

CLUMP. Low, irregular, quickly spreading, 6 × 18 in. (15 × 45 cm)

Prefers dappled shade but will take more sun in northern climates, and needs plenty of water. In the right location, this variety quickly forms a wide, dense mound. Sometimes known as *H.* 'Haku Chu Han'.

Hosta 'Silver Threads and Golden Needles'

LEAVES. Dull yellow margin, but the center varies immensely in different conditions, from light to mid-green with considerable lighter streaking and dotting to a misty chartreuse, 3½ × 2½ in. (9 × 6 cm)

CLUMP. Slow-growing, dense, 6 × 15 in. (15 × 38 cm)

A beautiful hosta that needs to be grown in good light but not in direct sun. Not easy to grow, requiring perfect light conditions to maintain the unique leaf pattern and coloration.

Hosta 'Striker'

LEAVES. Oval, mid-green with a crisp, slightly variable white margin, 4 × 2 in. (10 × 5 cm)

CLUMP. Fast-growing, irregular, quickly spreading, 9 × 20 in. (23 × 50 cm)

Undemanding. One of the best small variegated hostas that will do well anywhere. Similar to *H.* 'Little White Lines'.

Hosta 'Tweeny'

LEAVES. Oval, mid-green, slightly shiny and held on long petioles, 1½ × 1 in. (4 × 3 cm)

CLUMP. Loose and irregular, 3 × 10 in. (8 × 25 cm)

Grows best in a few hours of early morning sun. Rhizomatous habit leads to a very diffuse wandering mound of very small foliage.

Hosta 'Xanadu'

LEAVES. Narrowly oval, white with a wide blue-green margin, 4 × 2½ in. (10 × 6 cm)

CLUMP. Fairly fast-growing, tight, 6 × 12 in. (15 × 30 cm)

Grows well in good light in cooler climates and can quickly fill the corner of a trough or the back of a raised bed. Contrasting foliage makes it a standout in the dappled shade of a woodland walk.

Driftwood and hollowed logs

A delightful garden can easily be planted among pieces of driftwood or in a hollowed log. Suitable logs can often be found in forests or old woodpiles; a lucky find is a rotted log covered in moss. Over time, entire trees fall and begin to decay; and even they can be hollowed for additional planting interest for your smallest hostas.

If you are using driftwood as your base, fill in the gaps with a mixture of soil, pine bark fines or peat, and a particulate, such as builder's sand, turkey grit, or turface (see the list on page 29). The optimum percentages are 50 percent soil, 25 percent bark or peat, and 25 percent solids. This allows for good drainage, while ensuring the small roots don't dry out between watering.

If using a log, care must be taken that there are allowances for drainage. If the log is spongy enough, chop out your cavity (8 to 10 inches deep) with a hand pick or small hatchet. Fill the bottom 4 to 5 inches with gravel. If it is more solid, you can drill out your cavity, with deeper drilling to help with drainage. Fill the cavity with the soil mixture, and arrange your hostas before planting. Think of how the forest floor appears, and artfully aim to recreate that look. Additional interest can be achieved with moss, ferns, astilbes, thalictrums, and other shade-tolerant plants (see chapter five).

We had a tree come down in our yard several

A small fallen log planted with three miniature hostas.

The trunk of a fallen tree, hollowed out and planted with mini hostas in the garden of Mike and Libby Greanya, Jackson, Michigan.

years ago, and after chopping up what we could, we were left with the remainder of the roots attached to a section of trunk that was too big to saw ourselves and too expensive to have professionally removed. The solution? A planting opportunity! We dug out the area where the roots had come up from the ground until it was large enough to walk through, and planted the areas between the large roots with small hostas. It was a very interesting grotto area.

Hosta 'Cameo'

LEAVES. Broadly oval, mid-green with an irregular creamy white margin, often with a pleasing darker green-blue area where center and edge overlap, 1½ × 1½ in. (4 × 4 cm)

CLUMP. Tight, with a moderate growth rate, 4 × 8 in. (10 × 20 cm)

Early morning sun will bring out the sharp color contrasts. Also ideal for the small tray, ceramic bowl, or rock garden.

Hosta 'Change of Heart'

LEAVES. Heart-shaped, pale yellow with a wide white margin, 3 × 1½ in. (8 × 4 cm)

CLUMP. Loose, erect, 6 × 12 in. (15 × 30 cm)

A pretty but very delicate little variety that has done well planted in a log in a shady part of the woodland walk.

Hosta 'Lakeside Dimpled Darling'

LEAVES. Elliptic to oval, light green with a fairly wide cream to white margin, 3 × 2 in. (8 × 5 cm)
CLUMP. Fast-growing and loose, 4 × 12 in. (10 × 30 cm)

Also ideal for a window box, large trough, or the back of a raised bed.

Hosta 'Little Stiffy'

LEAVES. Spindle-shaped, bright yellow with good substance, 2½ × 1 in. (6 × 3 cm)
CLUMP. Tiny but very irregular, 3 × 7 in. (8 × 18 cm)

Although smaller than many otherwise similar yellow minis, it has better substance. Will do well in a small container or tray, and the color contrasts nicely with the dark wood of a tree stump.

Little hostas as edging plants

Some hostas grow so exuberantly they may be divided and divided again and will soon provide you with a living edge for your woodland walk or along the front of a raised bed. Hostas from the *H.* 'Lemon Lime' dynasty are excellent little hostas for this purpose. These hostas will look best if planted behind other natural edging material, such as small stones, small logs and tree branches, or upended flat rocks.

Again, when using small, very small, and mini hostas, the effect is best if everything is kept to scale. This is extended to the materials on your path. If using gravel, for example, the smallest pebbles will be more appealing than a coarser stone. If using mulch, a finer ground variety will look best.

A slight difficulty may arise when using these fast-growing hostas as edging plants where the light is not consistent the entire length of the border. Those plants that find themselves in better light will grow faster but the clump will be shorter, while those in shadier spots will grow more slowly but taller. With careful placement, this irregular growth pattern can be reduced.

Hosta 'Green Eyes', named by Herb Benedict in honor of his wife, Dorothy, edges a path in their Michigan garden.

Hosta 'Lemon Frost' and *H.* 'Twist of Lime' edging a woodland border.

Hosta 'Kabitan' edging the front of a raised bed.

Hosta 'Bitsy Green' and *H.* 'Bitsy Gold' planted together.

Hosta 'Bitsy Gold'

LEAVES. Long and narrow with some rippling, bright yellow, 5 × 1½ in. (13 × 4 cm)

CLUMP. Fairly fast-growing and loose, 7 × 18 in. (18 × 45 cm)

Needs plenty of water to grow well. Excessive direct sunlight may bleach the leaves, but it will do well in many situations, including bordering a path or raised bed and as a groundcover. Looks particularly nice alternating with *H.* 'Bitsy Green', the green-leafed version, along the edge of a path. *Hosta* 'Bitsy Blue' is the more-difficult-to-find blue version.

Hosta 'Carrie Ann'

LEAVES. Lance-shaped, light green with a narrow white margin, 3½ × 1½ in. (9 × 4 cm)

CLUMP. Fast-growing, neat, 6 × 15 in. (15 × 38 cm)

Takes quite a lot of sun and can be used as an edging plant in a woodland garden or in a raised bed. Flowers match margin for whiteness.

Hosta 'Cody'

LEAVES. Heart-shaped, shiny dark green, 3 × 2 in. (8 × 5 cm)

CLUMP. Tight, moderate to fast-growing, 5 × 10 in. (13 × 25 cm)

Good light and plentiful water in a well-drained soil will promote fast growth and good color, so also an ideal plant for raised beds and rockeries.

Hosta 'Feather Boa'

LEAVES. Oval, distinctively veined, very wavy, narrow and pointed, yellow turning to chartreuse early in the season, 3½ × 2 in. (9 × 5 cm)

CLUMP. Fast-growing and dense, 10 × 20 in. (25 × 50 cm)

Too much sun quickly turns this variety green, but it is an excellent plant for borders and as a groundcover. Bears attractive red seed pods. *Hosta* 'Chartreuse Wiggles' is very similar.

Hosta 'Gaijin'

LEAVES. Oval, slightly wavy and very pointed, mid- to bright green with a narrow yellow-gold margin, 2½ × 1½ in. (6 × 4 cm)

CLUMP. Fast-growing and dense, 6 × 12 in. (15 × 30 cm)

Best in dappled shade but a good edging plant for a border or pathway.

Hosta 'Ginko Craig'

LEAVES. Narrowly oval, mid-green with a narrow, slightly rippled white margin that broadens with maturity, 7 × 3 in. (18 × 8 cm)
CLUMP. Fast-growing and dense, 9 × 24 in. (23 × 60 cm)

Grows best in light to medium shade. A good border plant and suitable as a groundcover. This popular, well-established variety has many lookalikes, including *H.* 'Hi Ho Silver', *H.* 'Sarah Kennedy', *H.* 'Bunchoko', and *H.* 'Princess of Karafuto'.

Hosta 'Gold Drop'

LEAVES. Oval and flat, chartreuse to golden yellow, 2½ × 1½ in. (6 × 4 cm)

CLUMP. Irregular and fast-growing, 6 × 12 in. (15 × 30 cm)

Fairly sun-tolerant and a good plant for the border or path edge.

Hosta 'Green Eyes'

Hosta 'Yellow Eyes'

Hosta 'Green Eyes'

LEAVES. Lance-shaped, tapering, some rippling, pale yellow with a narrow mid-green margin, 3 × 1 in. (8 × 3 cm)

CLUMP. Fast-growing, dome-shaped, 5 × 12 in. (13 × 30 cm)

Although lacking in substance, this edger will take plenty of sun. *Hosta* 'Kabitan' is similar. *Hosta* 'Yellow Eyes', a sport, lacks the green margin.

Hosta 'Iced Lemon'

LEAVES. Lance-shaped, char-treuse to light green with a nar-row, crisp white margin, 3 × 1 in. (8 × 3 cm)

CLUMP. Low and dense, 5 × 11 in. (13 × 28 cm)

Grows well in good light. Ideal as an edging plant and in raised beds. Similar to *H.* 'Lemon Frost'.

Hosta 'Lemon Lime'

LEAVES. Oval when mature, char-treuse to greenish yellow, 3½ × 1½ in. (9 × 4 cm)

CLUMP. Very fast-growing, dense, 10 × 24 in. (25 × 60 cm)

A very easy-to-grow variety that will eventually get quite large if left undisturbed. Regular divi-sion yields plants to edge a bed or pathway. Also ideal for the wood-land garden and as a groundcover, but it should be kept out of strong sunlight.

Hosta 'Kabitan'

LEAVES. Lance-shaped, yellow turning chartreuse later in the season, with a narrow green margin, 5 × 2 in. (13 × 5 cm)

CLUMP. Fast-growing and loose, 10 × 15 in. (25 × 38 cm)

Emerges early in spring. In good light, this variety makes an excellent border plant to the front of a raised bed or along a path.

Hosta 'O'Harra'

LEAVES. Oblong, medium yellow turning chartreuse later in the season, 3 × 1½ in. (8 × 4 cm)

CLUMP. Low, tight, 7 × 20 in. (18 × 50 cm)

One of the better simple yellow varieties that grows well in the sun. Can be used as an edging plant or as a groundcover in a woodland garden.

Hosta 'Stiletto'

LEAVES. Lance-shaped, rippled, mid- to dark green with a narrow white margin, 5½ × 1½ in. (14 × 4 cm)

CLUMP. Fast-growing and tall, 12 × 24 in. (30 × 60 cm)

Grows well in almost any position and is ideal as an edging plant along a pathway or across the back of a raised bed. *Hosta* 'Wiggle Worms' is similar.

Hosta 'Traveler'

LEAVES. Narrow, ribbonlike, mid-green with a bright white, rippled margin, 5 × 1½ in. (13 × 4 cm)

CLUMP. Fast-growing, loose, and sometimes unruly, 8 × 18 in. (20 × 45 cm)

This quickly spreading hosta will do well bordering a bed or pathway in light to dappled shade.

Rockeries and screes

Most people are familiar with the concept of a rock garden, which is generally situated in full sun and contains small, alkaline-loving alpine plants. The same basic concept may be applied to a garden situated in a more shady area of the property and populated with small hostas and other plants that prefer slightly more acid soil. You may even be able to blend the two types of gardens—after all, even a sunny garden has a shady side—although given the different pH preferences, it might be more trouble than you bargain for.

A scree garden is meant to resemble the debris field at the bottom of a mountain. It is composed of gravels of varying sizes, although when combining a scree garden and small hostas, you will need to remember to consider the scale of the gravel material, or the plants may be overwhelmed. We combine rockeries and screes here because the plant material is compatible.

The rockery is built in a shady spot as too much sun is likely to damage shade-tolerant hostas and bleach out their colors.

A large rockery planted with little hostas and mulched with gravel to add color contrast and prevent splashback in the garden of Mike and Libby Greanya, Jackson, Michigan.

Hosta 'Pandora's Box', *H.* 'Tiny Tears', and *H.* 'Medusa' together with small companion plants enjoy the shade of a specially constructed hosta rockery.

Hosta 'Green Eyes' and *H.* 'Gum Drop' planted in a mixture of gravel grades on a gentle slope.

Hosta 'Crepe Soul'

LEAVES. Narrowly oval, green with a wide milky white margin, new leaves emerge with a rich yellow edge, 4 × 1 in. (10 × 3 cm)

CLUMP. Low, with a moderate growth rate, 6 × 15 in. (15 × 38 cm)

Nicely contrasting foliage. Grows well in light to full shade. Ideal for the rock garden and raised bed.

Hosta 'Daisy Doolittle'

LEAVES. Blue-green, sometimes mottled green-gray, with a creamy white variable-width margin, 2 × 1 in. (5 × 3 cm)

CLUMP. A slow-growing, low rosette, 2 × 6 in. (5 × 15 cm)

Grows better out of full sun and is ideal for the container, trough, and rock garden.

Hosta 'Hope'

LEAVES. Rounded, mid-green with a wide yellow-green margin, 2½ × 1½ in. (6 × 4 cm)

CLUMP. Neat, with a slow to moderate growth rate, 5 × 10 in. (13 × 25 cm)

Grows well in good light but is not vigorous. Excellent in a small tray or trough and in the rock garden.

Hosta 'Imp'

LEAVES. Lance-shaped, dark green with a narrow, creamy white margin that turns yellow as the season progresses, 2 × 1 in. (5 × 3 cm)

CLUMP. Loose in youth, tight when mature, 3 × 7 in. (8 × 18 cm)

This very small plant thrives in well-drained soil and can take plenty of sun in cooler climates. Ideal for a small tray or at the front of a raised bed as well as the shady side of a rock garden.

Hosta 'Lakeside Cricket'

LEAVES. Heart-shaped, creamy white turning ivory with an olive-green margin, sometimes flecked and spotted green, 1½ × 1 in. (4 × 3 cm)

CLUMP. Dense, upright rosette, 3 × 4 in. (8 × 10 cm)

This tiny plant needs special attention. Rain showers can cause mud and dirt to splash onto the underside of the leaves, causing problems. The very small rosettes look wonderful in a tray, trough, or rockery, where a gravel mulch can prevent splashback. Not easy to grow but worth the effort.

Hosta 'Lakeside Little Tuft'

LEAVES. Lance-shaped, very shiny with good substance, yellow-gold with a wide dark green margin, 4 × 1½ in. (10 × 4 cm)

CLUMP. Low and dense, slow to moderate growth rate, 5 × 12 in. (13 × 30 cm)

A growing habit very close to the ground means that a good mulch or gravel base may be necessary to prevent splashback.

Hosta 'Lakeside Zinger'

LEAVES. Oval, mid-green with a wide white margin that sometimes exhibits attractive green flecks, 3 × 2 in. (8 × 5 cm)

CLUMP. Fast-growing and neat, 7 × 9 in. (18 × 23 cm)

Will take some sun and grows well in practically any situation. The small mound it forms makes it ideal for the trough or tray as well as the rockery.

Hosta 'Limey Lisa'

LEAVES. Spoon-shaped, lime-green, darkening a little as the season progresses, 2½ × 2 in. (6 × 5 cm)

CLUMP. Fast-growing, tight, 8 × 21 in. (20 × 53 cm)

Needs good light but not direct sun except in cooler climates.

Ideal for containers, troughs, and the rockery, provided space is sufficient to accommodate its vigorous growth.

Hosta 'Paradise Sunset'

LEAVES. Oval, dark olive-green with a narrow bright yellow margin that darkens during the season, 2½ × 1½ in. (6 × 4 cm)

CLUMP. Low-growing and dense, 8 × 14 in. (20 × 35 cm)

Grows best in dappled shade. An ideal variety for rock gardens, sinks, and troughs. Leaves that lose their margin should be removed to prevent the whole plant's reverting to green.

Hosta 'Saishu Jima'

LEAVES. Long, narrow, and very rippled, glossy dark green, 3½ × 1 in. (9 × 3 cm)

CLUMP. Fast-growing, low, tight, spreading with maturity, 7 × 18 in. (18 × 45 cm)

Ideal for the border and raised bed, but smaller divisions make very good trough and rockery plants.

Hosta 'Teeny-weeny Bikini'

LEAVES. Lance-shaped, very variable in color, white to very pale green to yellow with a darker green margin, sometimes with streaking, 2½ × 1½ in. (6 × 4 cm)
CLUMP. Low and compact, 4 × 9 in. (10 × 23 cm)

The leaf centers often burn in strong sunshine. This small plant would be easily lost in any flowerbed but is ideally suited to the trough, tray, or rockery.

Hosta 'Yellow Submarine'

LEAVES. Long and narrow, heavily rippled, chartreuse to golden yellow, 6 × 1½ in. (15 × 4 cm)
CLUMP. Fairly fast-growing and loose, 9 × 18 in. (23 × 45 cm)

Grows well in a position where it gets some sunshine. It will look good in a large container, raised bed, or rockery.

Container planting

Small hostas thrive in containers. In fact, some of the smallest, most finicky hostas actually are better off in a pot, where soil, water, and growing conditions can be monitored and manipulated. Happily, where not everyone can manage a garden, we all can manage container planting.

Many newly purchased hostas will be quite small and take several years to reach their mature size. During their first one or two seasons, therefore, they are very suitable for planting in a wide variety of pots, bowls, and other containers. The advantages to putting new hostas in containers are many: besides being more easily enjoyed, the newly arrived plants can be given tender loving care, overwintered effortlessly, and—after a couple of seasons—moved

One hundred containerized hostas—some arranged on iron étagères, others in various pots and bowls—on our small deck.

out into a garden location, thus freeing up a special pot for another new acquisition.

The very first consideration when selecting a container for a small hosta, no matter where you may garden, is drainage. Although hostas do need water, the smallest varieties, with their tiny roots, will not tolerate "wet feet." It is crucial, therefore, that care be taken that the selected container have adequate drainage holes so that water drains through, and that the roots be able to receive both the water and the oxygen they need. If there are no drainage holes, the next question to ask is whether you will be able to drill some. Some of the better nurseries selling plant containers will drill drainage holes for you, but in most cases, it is not a difficult task to accomplish on your own with the right drill bit, some tape over the area being drilled (to discourage cracks from forming and the drill from slipping), and nerves of steel.

Another view of our containerized hostas, some alone, some with companions, showing how happily they will grow in a wide range of pots and found objects.

Hostas, even the smallest, will do best if they have at least 5 inches of planting mix for their roots, so depth is the next important criteria. Look for trays and containers with that minimal depth, and with straight, rather than sloping, sides. The slope will mean that plant material around the edge has less room for their roots, and watering may also be a problem. This is not to say that you can never plant a mini hosta in less soil depth, but if you do, special care needs to be paid to watering. A tiny hosta will live happily in a very shallow bowl for several years; small hostas will probably require transplanting annually.

For those gardeners who deal with long, cold winters, yet another important consideration when selecting a container for little hostas is whether or not the container is frost-proof. In our own garden, we have been unhappily surprised more than once in the spring when uncovering our hosta collection to find some plants lying in a pile of pottery shards! Your nurseryman may or may not be a reliable authority when it comes to determining how a container will weather. When in doubt, consider bringing the container inside to an unheated garage or shed. Allowing the container to go into the colder months on the dry side will also help a marginal pot to remain intact.

Another way to deal with a container that may not be suitable for wintering outside, is not to actually plant *in* it, but rather plant your hosta in a nursery pot slightly smaller than the ornamental container. The potted hosta is then dropped inside and the edges of the pot are covered with mulch to disguise the deception. The inner pot can be removed for the winter and the container safely stored or turned upside down till spring.

When planting in a container, remember to use a light and airy potting mix, not garden soil. Work in some type of particulate with your planting mix as well, again at the optimum 25 percent of volume, for air spaces to allow the movement of water and oxygen. With the smallest hostas, soil texture is far more important than with larger ones. A clay soil is much too dense for their more delicate root system, and so a good soil mixture is probably the best guarantee your potted hostas will thrive. Expert growers of small hostas have their own formulas for the perfect potting soil. These can be as simple as pure composted or triple-ground pine bark (commercially available, but easiest to find in the southern United States), or as complicated as a mixture of grit and ProMix, a good sterile potting soil. Again, we don't particularly care for mixes that contain perlite, but we have to admit it is lightweight and does provide the necessary air space in the soil. In our experience, it is rather like garden dandruff, but if you're not bothered by its appearance, it's probably the way to go. See chapter three for more details on particulates, ProMix, perlite, and more.

As small hostas are comfortable and lovely in containers, the next question is, where to put these containers to maximum effect—never forgetting, of course, that the amount of light available should be a consideration. Hostas can be arranged on the edge of steps, on a balcony, on a patio or deck. The impact is particularly effective if you use similar containers, but a diverse mixture of pots and bowls may add to the visual charm, and collecting unusual pots may become as much fun as collecting little hostas. Recently we managed to fit one hundred containerized little hostas

The advantage of having hostas with similar properties together in a container is that they are easy to move to safety if frost threatens. This glazed bowl holds "early emergers": *H.* 'Verkade's One', *H.* 'Green with Envy', *H.* 'Kabitan', and *H.* 'Little Miss Magic'—with a dash of dianthus and lamium for a shock of color.

around a deck measuring less than 10 feet by 15 feet, and we still had room to entertain.

Gorgeous and charming art pottery containers not only showcase your small hostas but are themselves enhanced by a careful selection of just the right plant—or plants. (We have a dark raku glaze bowl planted with a very bright yellow hosta that will make you swoon.) Since this type of container is most likely not frost-proof, those who live in the north will either need to plant the hosta in another container set into the pottery, or have a plan for overwintering inside.

An interesting and inexpensive source of art pottery is your local nursery's bonsai section. There you will find small pots and trays especially made for miniature plants. When using bonsai containers, diligent attention must be paid to watering, as the more shallow depth will not hold sufficient moisture to keep the roots from drying. They may also need to be watered with a thin-spouted watering can or a gentle sprinkler type to prevent displacing all the soil with a rush of water. We have quite a few hostas planted in various bonsai pots and trays; we tend to favor the unglazed types, which seem to complement the plant more than the shiny ones, and find that a

A shallow clay bowl containing three little hostas, each of a different color and form, is used as the centerpiece of the hosta collection on our deck.

mulch of polished black stone looks especially nice.

If you have a collection of potted hostas to display, there are many types of outdoor shelving, some made especially for displaying plants, to consider—from ornate iron étagères and corner what-not shelves to functional but lovely bakers' racks. Thus displayed, your plants will have a couple of advantages: they are shown at a level where they can be enjoyed, and they are in one place for watering. What's more, your arrangement can be interspersed with other potted plants (dwarf trees and conifers, small orchids) or brightened up with annuals. Your hostas can even share the space with a collection of rocks, geodes, or garden gnomes.

Found objects—drilled bowls, shells, teacups—are fun to plant. We like to browse garage sales and flea markets for unique containers for hostas:

• Interesting china or ceramic bowls. Drill fine holes in the bottom; if drilling is absolutely not possible, you may still be able to use a container with adequate depth by first putting several inches of aquarium gravel, aquarium charcoal, or fine stone in the bottom. This will prevent the roots from sitting in a pool of rancid water.

• Shells. We've seen large resin shells used as hosta planters, but there is no reason a real shell could not be used if drainage is respected.

• Teacups. A lovely Victorian-flavored vignette is an arrangement of mismatched garage sale teacups, planted with hostas, set on a bistro table.

• A child's wagon can hold an entire mini hosta garden. In the one we saw, rust holes precluded drilling, and the sides were just the right height for a good 8 inches of soil for the hostas. Added were some trailing ivies, a few mossy rocks, and a small weeping laceleaf Japanese maple—and the effect was fabulous. A similar container would be an old garden wheelbarrow. An obvious advantage to these wheeled containers is portability.

The bottom line is to be creative and have fun. Almost anything can be a planting container for little hostas. The following hostas are especially well suited to life in a container.

Hosta 'Alakazaam'

LEAVES. Very narrow and straplike, green with a wide and heavily rippled yellow-gold margin that turns creamy white later in the season, 5 × 1 in. (13 × 3 cm)

CLUMP. Moderately fast-growing and loose, 7 × 12 in. (18 × 30 cm)

Needs morning sun and once established will grow well. Ideal for pots and containers.

Hosta 'Apple Court'

LEAVES. Very twisted and curled, white with a wide bright green margin, 4 × 1½ in. (10 × 4 cm)

CLUMP. Slow-growing, tight, and untidy, 6 × 12 in. (15 × 30 cm)

Difficult but worth the effort. It needs to be planted in dappled shade in a pot where it will get special care and the unusual foliage can be appreciated. *Hosta* 'Kiwi Spearmint' is similar.

Hosta 'Awesome'

LEAVES. Elongated teardrop, slightly rippled and folded, medium olive-green, 1½ × 1 in. (4 × 3 cm)

CLUMP. Very small, flat rosette, 2 × 4 in. (5 × 10 cm)

This early emerger will require care. Morning sun is best and plenty of water desirable. So small, this little plant is only really suitable for the ceramic container or bowl.

Hosta 'Blue Mouse Ears'

LEAVES. Almost round, flat, good medium blue, held high on thick petioles, 2½ × 2½ in. (6 × 6 cm)

CLUMP. Moderately fast-growing, fairly upright and loose, 9 × 12 in. (23 × 30 cm)

The flowerbuds are attractively balloonlike. This tough blue will look good in a container or trough.

Hosta 'Boyz Toy'

LEAVES. Heart-shaped, chartreuse in early spring with faint pinkish red leaf tips, turning bright yellow later in the season as the red fades, 3½ × 2 in. (9 × 5 cm)

CLUMP. Fast-growing and compact, 6 × 12 in. (15 × 30 cm)

This pretty plant deserves its own container. A few hours of direct sunlight each day will bring out the best color.

Hosta 'Cat and Mouse'

LEAVES. Round, yellow-green with a blue-green margin, 2 × 1½ in. (5 × 4 cm)

CLUMP. Very small and flat, 3 × 6 in. (8 × 15 cm)

Good light and a well-drained soil encourages good growth. It will be interesting to see if this plant gets bigger as it matures.

Hosta 'Cherish'

LEAVES. Heart-shaped, creamy yellow, turning to white, with a wide blue-green margin, 2½ × 1½ in. (6 × 4 cm)

CLUMP. Slow-growing, compact, 8 × 12 in. (20 × 30 cm)

To maintain a healthy growth rate in cool climates, it needs plenty of sunshine.

Hosta 'Collector's Choice'

LEAVES. Oval, mid-green with a hint of blue, 2 × 1 in. (5 × 3 cm)

CLUMP. A tight mound, 5 × 16 in. (13 × 40 cm)

Keep out of bright sunshine to maintain that hint of blue. Ideal in a collection of small hostas in a container.

Hosta 'Cookie Crumbs'

LEAVES. Teardrop-shaped, mid-green with a wide white margin that usually turns yellow as it matures, 2 × 1½ in. (5 × 4 cm)

CLUMP. Neat, low, and slightly loose, 5 × 16 in. (13 × 40 cm)

Will take early morning sun and always looks good in a bowl, pot, or trough.

Hosta 'Crepe Suzette'

LEAVES. Elliptic, dark green with a cream, sometimes turning white, margin, 5 × 2 in. (13 × 5 cm)

CLUMP. Slow-growing, loose, and fairly flat, 8 × 15 in. (20 × 38 cm)

Needs good light. This variety will make a colorful addition to a collection of potted hostas. *Hosta* 'Cream Cheese' is similar.

Hosta 'Dawn'

LEAVES. Almost round, dull yellow, 3 × 2 in. (8 × 5 cm)

CLUMP. Fast-growing, 8 × 15 in. (20 × 38 cm)

The dull yellow contrasts well with green and blue companions in a trough or bowl. Should not be grown in full sun.

Hosta 'Duchess'

LEAVES. Heart-shaped, pointed and slightly rippled, mid-green with a wide, irregular dirty-white margin, 4 × 2 in. (10 × 5 cm)

CLUMP. Mounded, 6 × 12 in. (15 × 30 cm)

A pretty plant needing good light that will provide plenty of color contrast in a mixed planting. Ideal for the larger pot or container. Expect it to grow larger than the declared size.

Hosta 'Ellie Bee'

LEAVES. Lance-shaped, pointed and slightly wavy, dull yellow, 4½ × 2½ in. (11 × 6 cm)

CLUMP. Fairly fast-growing and dense, 6 × 10 in. (15 × 25 cm)

A very pretty plant that provides excellent color contrast in a mixed planting. Will enjoy early morning sun and look good in a pot or container.

Hosta 'Extreme'

LEAVES. Broadly oval, blue-green with a wide, darker blue margin, the two colors divided by a paler, almost white line of irregular width, 4 × 3 in. (10 × 8 cm)

CLUMP. Slow-growing, fairly tight rosette, 8 × 13 in. (20 × 32 cm)

This cultivar will need exactly the right amount of sun to bring out the best coloration of its very unusual leaf pattern. It is therefore best in a pot or container that can be moved around until the best spot is found.

Hosta 'Fantasy Island'

LEAVES. Elliptic to oval, narrow white center with a wide dark green margin, 4 × 2½ in. (10 × 6 cm)

CLUMP. Fast-growing and loose, 7 × 12 in. (18 × 30 cm)

Best in dappled shade but will take some direct sunlight. A colorful variety that would make an excellent feature plant in a containerized collection.

Hosta 'Heart and Soul'

LEAVES. Heart-shaped, light green with a mid-green variable-width margin, 3 × 3½ in. (8 × 9 cm)

CLUMP. Well-proportioned, with a moderate growth rate, 10 × 15 in. (25 × 38 cm)

The light green leaf center will turn yellow in a sunny location. Ideal for a raised bed or large container.

Hosta 'Illicit Affair'

LEAVES. Almost round and slightly wavy, lime to mid-green with a bright gold margin, 3½ × 2½ in. (9 × 6 cm)

CLUMP. Fairly fast-growing and flattish, 6 × 12 in. (15 × 30 cm)

Will enjoy morning sun in cooler climates. Ideally planted in a small container until it matures.

Hosta 'Lakeside Down Sized'

LEAVES. Narrow, tapering, slightly rippled, greenish yellow with a narrow white margin, 2½ × 1 in. (6 × 3 cm)

CLUMP. Fast-growing, crowded and untidy, 4 × 9 in. (10 × 23 cm)

Will do well in almost any situation, but because it lacks substance and is therefore vulnerable to slugs and snails, this cultivar fares better planted in a container.

Hosta 'Lakeside Zing Zang'

LEAVES. White to creamy white with numerous irregular dark green flecks and blotches, 1½ × ¾ in. (4 × 2 cm)

CLUMP. Upright, 3 × 6 in. (8 × 15 cm)

Difficult to grow without the exact amount of beneficial light (establish by experimentation), so will do better in a container that is easily moved to the best available location.

Hosta 'Lime Fizz'

LEAVES. Narrow and pointed, light green with a narrow bright white margin, 4 × 1 in. (10 × 3 cm)

CLUMP. Fairly loose but neat, 6 × 12 in. (15 × 30 cm)

A fast-growing cultivar given good light and plenty of water.

Hosta 'Little Jay'

LEAVES. Narrow and tapering, widening to oval with maturity, creamy white with a variable blue-green margin, 3½ × 1 in. (9 × 3 cm)
CLUMP. Flat rosette, eventually an irregular mound, 5 × 13 in. (13 × 32 cm)

Too much sun in warmer climates may burn out the center of this pretty variety, the best and most attractive of this type and ideal for containers and troughs.

Hosta 'Peanut'

LEAVES. Oval, seersuckered and pebbled, creamy white with an irregular and sometimes streaky mid- to dark green margin, 3½ × 2 in. (9 × 5 cm)
CLUMP. Unruly and somewhat flat, 6 × 10 in. (15 × 25 cm)

In good light the leaf margins diversify into many different shades of green. The small clump size and low growth habit make it ideal for the trough and bowl.

Hosta 'Pinwheel'

LEAVES. Oval, very twisted, slightly folded, ivory white with an irregular green margin, 4 × 1½ in. (10 × 4 cm)

CLUMP. Upright, 7 × 10 in. (18 × 25 cm)

A delicate plant that needs to be carefully tended until it matures and thereafter planted in light shade in a larger container or raised bed.

Hosta 'Snow Mouse'

LEAVES. Almost round, very thick, slightly pointed, brilliant white with a wide blue-green margin, 2½ × 2 in. (6 × 5 cm)

CLUMP. Slow-growing, flattish, 7 × 12 in. (18 × 30 cm)

Will take some sun and is ideal for a ceramic container. A good gravel mulch will prevent splashback and better show off this pretty plant.

Hosta 'Subtlety'

LEAVES. Rounded, pale to mid green with a very variable wide yellow margin, 4 × 3 in. (10 × 8 cm) **CLUMP**. Slow-growing, fairly flat and tight, 10 × 20 in. (25 × 50 cm)

A beautiful hosta that needs just the right amount of light to bring out the subtle variegation. Ideal for a small container that can be moved around until the right spot is found.

Hosta 'Tickle Me Pink'

LEAVES. Oval, bright gold with a slightly rippled margin and a sharp tip that shows a tinge of pink in early spring, 5 × 3½ in. (13 × 9 cm) **CLUMP**. Low, circular, 8 × 20 in. (20 × 50 cm)

This plant needs plenty of sun to produce that bright yellow coloration and bring out the red in the petioles and leaves. Will look good in a container or trough.

Hosta 'Tiny Dancer'

LEAVES. Oval, chartreuse to lime-green with a narrow white margin, 2½ × 1½ in. (6 × 4 cm)

CLUMP. Low, circular, 5 × 10 in. (13 × 25 cm)

Needs early morning sun in cooler climates and dappled shade further south. Makes an ideal container plant.

Hosta 'Trifecta'

LEAVES. Oval, creamy white with a wide margin that is a mixture of green and yellow toward the middle of the leaf and green at the edge, 5 × 4 in. (13 × 10 cm)

CLUMP. Loose, 8 × 12 in. (20 × 30 cm)

Does not enjoy direct sun in warmer climates and needs plenty of water while it becomes established. A good variety for containers and bowls.

Troughs, trays, and similar large containers

Troughs, once the signature of fussy alpine gardens, have come center stage as a vehicle for small gardens of all types. The notion of planting in stone troughs came from England around the turn of the last century, when farmers began replacing their stone horse troughs with metal containers. Gardeners saw the value of the large, discarded vessels, which could be had for little or nothing. Now you would be lucky to find one of these true stone troughs, but there are alternatives.

Tufa is a type of porous rocklike substance formed when water evaporates from lime-rich areas, leaving behind calcite. Alpine gardeners worship the stuff and it is wonderful, but not necessarily for little hostas due to the high

Part of our collection of concrete and hypertufa troughs arranged in front of a stone wall.

alkaline content. For our purposes, hypertufa is actually a better choice. Hypertufa is a manmade approximation of the natural tufa substance and can be shaped into any form you wish. Most growers of small, very small, and mini hostas prefer to make alpine-type troughs and bowls, either classically shaped into a sizable rectangle or free-formed. Many recipes are available in your local library and on the Internet, and we encourage you to try your hand. One clever trick we learned: instead of buying expensive nylon fibers for stability and weather resistance, cut up and disassemble some inexpensive nylon rope.

A hypertufa mixture can also be mudded onto the outside of a discarded porcelain sink (first primed with a bonding agent). The mixture of peat, cement, and sand, mixed to a

Part of Sandra Bond's award-winning collection of alpine bowls, planted with little hostas.

sticky but firm consistency, is layered on the outside and partially down the inside of the sink. After curing, yogurt or buttermilk can be applied to attract moss for an aged appearance. If you are working with a larger sink, you should probably decide on the final placement and build in situ.

Among the chief catalysts for growing small hostas in trays and bowls were the artful displays created by Sandra Bond, garden designer and owner of Goldbrook Nursery in Suffolk, England. Year after year, her arrangements of small hostas won her gold medals at the RHS Chelsea Flower Show and inspired a love of small hostas in many gardeners.

A small hypertufa tray cleverly planted with small hostas. The yellow leaves of the single *H.* 'Goldbrook Grace' contrast effectively with the shiny green leaves of the other little hostas including *H.* 'Itsy Bitsy Spider', *H.* 'Tongue Twister', and *H.* 'Chabo Unazuki'.

This tray is planted with hostas with similarly colored leaves. They include *H.* 'Pinwheel', *H.* 'Oreo Cream', *H.* 'Striker', *H.* 'Manzo', and *H.* 'Lakeside Dimpled Darling'.

Hosta 'Blue Ice'

LEAVES. Almost round, with very good substance, mid-blue, 4 × 3½ in. (10 × 9 cm)

CLUMP. A low, flat rosette, very slow-growing, 5 × 12 in. (13 × 30 cm)

The exceptional blue leaf color can be maintained only by growing this plant out of direct sunlight. The growth rate makes it ideal for the trough and tray.

Hosta 'Blue Mouse Ears Supreme'

LEAVES. Rounded, blue-green streaked with yellow and cream, 2 × 1½ in. (5 × 4 cm)

CLUMP. Low and moderately fast-growing, 6 × 10 in. (15 × 25 cm)

Will appreciate some sun. An ideal plant for a trough, container, or the front of a raised bed.

Hosta 'Cat's Eye'

LEAVES. Oval, yellow, turning creamy white later in the season, with an irregular mid-green margin, 2 × 1 in. (5 × 3 cm)

CLUMP. Low, flat, fairly dense rosette, 3 × 12 in. (8 × 30 cm)

Early examples of this variety were difficult to grow, but a more robust strain seems to have been established. An excellent plant for the trough and tray that will need time to establish.

Hosta 'Chabo Unazuki'

LEAVES. Lance-shaped, pointed, dark green, held low on long petioles, 5 × 2 in. (13 × 5 cm)

CLUMP. Round, flat, and loose, 6 × 14 in. (15 × 35 cm)

Will do best in early morning sun. Dark green foliage will look good against light-colored mulch, which will show through the diffuse mound.

Hosta 'Country Mouse'

LEAVES. Heart-shaped, blue-green with a pure white margin, 2 × 2 in. (5 × 5 cm)

CLUMP. Slow-growing and flattish, 3 × 6 in. (8 × 15 cm)

Growth rate and strikingly contrasting color make this a perfect hosta for a small alpine tray, trough, or large container.

Hosta 'Frosted Mouse Ears'

LEAVES. Almost round, blue-green with a wide creamy white margin, 2½ × 2 in. (6 × 5 cm)

CLUMP. Slow-growing and flattish, 7 × 12 in. (18 × 30 cm)

Will take some sun and is ideal for a large container or alpine tray. This plant suffers greatly from splashback and needs a firm mulch to keep the leaves clean.

Hosta 'Junior Miss'

LEAVES. Elliptic, shiny dark green with a wide whitish yellow margin, 4 × 2 in. (10 × 5 cm)

CLUMP. A fairly fast-growing small rosette, 6 × 10 in. (15 × 25 cm)

The reflective leaf surface allows this cultivar to take some early morning sun. Good in a trough or at the front of a raised bed. *Hosta* 'Lookin' Pretty' is very similar.

Hosta 'Kinakafu Otome'

LEAVES. Oval, pointed, and slightly wavy, pale yellow with a light green margin in spring, turning mid-green later in the season, 3 × 2 in. (8 × 5 cm)

CLUMP. Fairly fast-growing, maturing to a tight mound, 5 × 18 in. (13 × 45 cm)

Too much sun soon results in loss of variegation. Ideal, therefore, for a container that can be moved around until the best location is found.

Hosta 'Kinbotan'

LEAVES. Oval, thick, mid-green with a narrow golden yellow margin that turns green as the season progresses, 2 × 1 in. (5 × 3 cm)

CLUMP. Fairly fast-growing, low, compact, 6 × 15 in. (15 × 38 cm)

Sometimes difficult to grow, but it can take a little sun. Neat habit makes it excellent for the trough and container.

Hosta 'Lakeside Little Gem'

LEAVES. Rounded, glossy, dark to mid-green, 3 × 2 in. (8 × 5 cm)

CLUMP. Neat and architectural, 5 × 10 in. (13 × 25 cm)

This very pretty small plant provides excellent color contrast with more showy companions in a tray or trough. Early morning sun will maintain a rich, dark green color.

Hosta 'Little Caesar'

LEAVES. Broadly lance-shaped, creamy white with a wide green rippled margin, 3 × 2 in. (8 × 5 cm)

CLUMP. Fast-growing and loose, 5 × 12 in. (13 × 30 cm)

In good light quickly forms an irregular mound. The leaves of young plants show a distinct twist. Ideal for troughs and bowls. Similar to H. 'Medusa' and H. 'Apple Court'.

Hosta 'Little Treasure'

LEAVES. Narrow and slightly twisted, creamy white with medium blue-green margin, 4½ × 1½ in. (11 × 4 cm)

CLUMP. Low, circular rosette, 5 × 11 in. (13 × 28 cm)

A fairly fast growth rate can be achieved with morning sun followed by dappled shade. Good in a trough or tray.

Hosta 'Margie Weissenberger'

LEAVES. Heart-shaped, folded and wavy, blue-green, 3 × 1 in. (8 × 3 cm)

CLUMP. Fast-growing and neat, 5 × 12 in. (13 × 30 cm)

Grows well in dappled shade; too much bright sun will quickly turn the leaves green.

Hosta '**Mighty Mouse**'

LEAVES. Rounded, slightly pointed, dull blue-green with a pale yellow margin, fading to white, 3 × 3 in. (8 × 8 cm)

CLUMP. Moderately fast-growing and flat, 4 × 8 in. (10 × 20 cm)

Does best in early morning sun and dappled shade. An ideal cultivar for the tray and trough.

Hosta '**Muffie**'

LEAVES. Oval to rounded, mid-green with a wide creamy white margin, 3 × 2 in. (8 × 5 cm)

CLUMP. Fairly fast-growing and dense, 8 × 12 in. (20 × 30 cm)

Best in morning sun. Neat habit makes it ideal for the large container, alpine tray, and small raised bed.

Hosta 'Orphan Annie'

LEAVES. Widely elliptic, arching, with a distinct tip, olive-green with a wide, irregular bright white margin, 2 × 1 in. (5 × 3 cm)
CLUMP. Fairly fast-growing and upright, 3 × 7 in. (8 × 18 cm)

Needs special care but once mature will do well in a container or trough.

Hosta '**Pandora's Box**'

LEAVES. Heart-shaped, bright white with an irregular blue-green margin, 2½ × 3 in. (6 × 8 cm)
CLUMP. Slow-growing, dense, 8 × 12 in. (20 × 30 cm)

The large white area makes this hosta a challenge to grow. It needs just the right amount of light: in cool climates, it can take a whole morning of sun but much less in warmer climes. Success is more certain if you grow it in a tray or trough for a few years before transferring to the garden. Once established, it makes a very striking, tight clump of contrasting foliage. Reversions are common: keep a vigilant watch for fully green leaves and remove them quickly. Will look good as the centerpiece of a *H.* 'Baby Bunting' collection.

Hosta 'Sitting Pretty'

LEAVES. Elliptic, creamy white to yellow with a wide mid-green margin, 6 × 2½ in. (15 × 6 cm)

CLUMP. Slow-growing, flat rosette, 6 × 15 in. (15 × 38 cm)

Demands morning sun and good drainage. Ideal for the larger trough and raised bed.

Hosta 'Surprised by Joy'

LEAVES. Narrow and wavy, creamy white with an irregular, streaky green margin, 3½ × 2 in. (9 × 5 cm)

CLUMP. Loose and fairly fast-growing, 6 × 12 in. (15 × 30 cm)

Can take a few hours of sun in cooler climates. Looks good in troughs, trays, and toward the front of a raised bed.

Hosta 'Teaspoon'

LEAVES. Almost round, cupped, mid-green, held on long petioles, 3 × 3 in. (8 × 8 cm)

CLUMP. Neat, round, fast-growing and upward-facing, 10 × 22 in. (25 × 55 cm)

Grows well in light shade. Ideal for the larger tray or trough.

Hosta 'Tongue Twister'

LEAVES. Very pointed and very twisted, good substance, shiny dark green, 6 × 2 in. (15 × 5 cm)

CLUMP. Upright, forming an unusual rosette, 8 × 18 in. (20 × 45 cm)

Will appreciate early morning sun and looks good in a trough or tray until late in the season.

Hosta 'X-ray'

LEAVES. Lance-shaped, white to very pale green with a narrow mid-green margin, 7 × 1 in. (18 × 3 cm)
CLUMP. Upright, with a moderate growth rate, 8 × 15 in. (20 × 38 cm)

Even in poor light, the light green leaves darken as the season progresses. The upright habit makes it an excellent plant for the back of a mixed collection in a large trough.

Window boxes

A window box is an excellent place for your small hostas, as long as there is some shade to keep your plants from burning. These boxes are normally fixed to the wall below a window but may be attached to any plain wall or simply rested on a wide sill. If you purchase a window box, look for one that is at least 8 inches deep. Again, we recommend the small hosta soil mixture of 50/25/25 (see chapter three). Styrofoam peanuts or aquarium gravel can be placed as a first layer, especially if your window box has no drainage holes. This will allow water to pool below the reach of the roots.

For a spectacular effect in your window boxes, follow the rule of "thriller, spiller, and filler." That is, choose hostas with pizzazz either in pattern or shape. Upright hostas, such as H. 'Little Caesar', will look great, as will vividly patterned or especially brightly colored plants like H. 'Quarter Note'. Any hosta with red or purple petioles is especially choice in a window box; the elevated siting will allow you to appreciate this often hidden feature. Small hostas that cascade are also a good choice. Add a spiller like *Euphorbia* 'Diamond Frost' or a small-leafed euonymus, and fill in the gaps with low or trailing companion plants to tie it all together.

A window box doesn't need a window and can be used to brighten up an otherwise plain wall.

A group of green and white hostas planted with white-flowering *Euphorbia* 'Diamond Frost' in a strong wooden window box.

Hosta 'Bedford Rise and Shine'

LEAVES. Oval, deeply veined, shiny mid-green with a yellow-white edge and red petioles, 5 × 2 in. (13 × 5 cm)

CLUMP. Fast-growing and densely leaved, 8 × 12 in. (20 × 30 cm)

Needs morning sun to bring promote good leaf and petiole color; the bright petioles especially are more easily seen in an elevated position such as a window box or raised bed.

Hosta 'Coconut Custard'

LEAVES. Oval, slightly wavy and rippled, pale yellow darkening to light green, with purple petioles, 4 × 2 in. (10 × 5 cm)

CLUMP. A neat, tight rosette, 5 × 12 in. (13 × 30 cm)

Will take plenty of sun in cooler climates. Also ideal for the trough or tray, where the color contrasts well with darker companions, and the petioles are more easily seen.

Hosta 'Dragon Tails'

LEAVES. Lance-shaped, heavily rippled and tapering to a fine point, yellow, 5 × 1 in. (13 × 3 cm)

CLUMP. Arching, tight, dome-shaped, 7 × 14 in. (18 × 35 cm)

Grows best in light shade. Looks good against dark mulch and is ideal for the trough or window or deck box, where it can be planted toward the edge so that the arching foliage drapes over and disguises the lip. *Hosta* 'Chartreuse Wiggles' is very similar but has slightly longer leaves that turn darker late in the season.

Hosta 'First Mate'

LEAVES. Narrow, pointed, wavy and twisted, creamy yellow with a dark green margin, 8 × 2 in. (20 × 5 cm)

CLUMP. Irregular, with a moderate growth rate, 10 × 21 in. (25 × 53 cm)

The very thick substance of the leaves allows this plant to take more sun than expected. Good in a raised bed and window box, where it can be planted to spill over the edge.

Hosta 'Lizard Lick'

LEAVES. Long and narrow with good substance and a slightly rippled margin, green, 7 × 1½ in. (18 × 4 cm)

CLUMP. Fast-growing, dome-shaped, 12 × 20 in. (30 × 50 cm)

Grows well even in poor light, so also ideal for the back of a raised bed, in a shady woodland border, or even as a specimen plant in a pale ceramic container.

Hosta 'Quarter Note'

LEAVES. Oval, shiny dark green with pinkish petioles and an irregular white margin tinged with yellow, 2½ × 1½ in. (6 × 4 cm)

CLUMP. Neat, with a moderate growth rate, 7 × 15 in. (18 × 38 cm)

Grows best in dappled shade.

This very colorful cultivar needs to be in a raised position to properly appreciate the petioles and red flower scapes.

Hosta 'Satin Bloomers'

LEAVES. Elliptic, dark green with a very narrow pale yellow margin, 5 × 3 in. (13 × 8 cm)

CLUMP. Fast-growing and dense, 10 × 20 in. (25 × 50 cm)

A tall-growing small hosta that will do well in a window or deck box or the back of a raised bed.

Hosta 'The Razor's Edge'

LEAVES. Long and narrow, heavily rippled, mid-green with white back and red petioles, 5 × 1½ in. (13 × 4 cm)

CLUMP. Loose and upright, 8 × 18 in. (20 × 45 cm)

Grows well in good light with plenty of water. An ideal hosta for the window box, where the bright petioles can more easily be seen and the white backs of the leaves occasionally glimpsed.

Hosta 'X-rated'

LEAVES. Very ribbonlike and slightly rippled, white with a narrow dark green margin, 6 × ½ in. (15 × 1½ cm)

CLUMP. Upright, with a moderate growth rate, 7 × 10 in. (18 × 25 cm)

Best in dappled shade. The leaf center remains white throughout the season. Also good for a rockery, tub, or mixed planting.

Deck boxes

Deck or patio boxes are exaggerated window boxes, meant to decorate the perimeter of the space. Because they are, therefore, much longer than window boxes, there is an opportunity to repeat a design or to plant a collection in one place. The same planting rules apply as for window boxes; drainage is important, as is planting medium.

Deck and patio boxes are useful containers in which to plant newly acquired little hostas close to the house. They may also be used as a "hospital area" or as a special place in which to plant a hosta that needs some tender loving care, or requires watching for one reason or another. You will still have the pleasure of using the plant in a combination, while keeping it close for extra attention.

Deck boxes can be fixed on the outside of the deck or arranged in front of the lowest deck rail, and in either case will provide an extra opportunity to plant small hostas and companion plants with different textures and form.

Hosta 'Dixie Chickadee'

LEAVES. Elliptic, very pointed, shiny creamy yellow with many green spots and flecks and a wide dark green margin, 3½ × 2 in. (9 × 5 cm)

CLUMP. Moderately fast-growing, dense, 5 × 12 in. (13 × 30 cm)

Grows well in part sun or dappled shade. A good variety for the deck box and raised bed.

Hosta 'Fire Island'

LEAVES. Rounded, bright yellow in spring, darkening as the season progresses, with red petioles, 5½ × 4 in. (14 × 10 cm)

CLUMP. Upright, with a moderate growth rate, 10 × 18 in. (25 × 45 cm)

A prominent raised position in a fairly sunny spot will display both the bright foliage and the striking petioles. Ideal for the deck or window box and raised bed.

Hosta 'Gosan Hildegarde'

LEAVES. Narrow and pointed, dull yellow-green, 6 × 1½ in. (15 × 4 cm)

CLUMP. Upright and dense, 8 × 10 in. (20 × 25 cm)

Too much sun will quickly turn this plant pale green. Ideal for the raised bed, container, and deck box.

Hosta 'Hideout'

LEAVES. Broadly lance-shaped, shiny, slightly rippled and twisted, bright white with a wide dark green margin, 4 × 2 in. (10 × 5 cm)

CLUMP. Fairly fast-growing, 6 × 11 in. (15 × 28 cm)

Needs morning sun and plenty of water. An ideal trough or deck box plant that will also look good at the front of a raised bed.

Hosta 'Lakeside Scamp'

LEAVES. Oval, pale blue-green with a narrow white margin, 2 × 1 in. (5 × 3 cm)

CLUMP. Flat, round rosette, 3 × 9 in. (8 × 23 cm)

A little hosta that will grow anywhere in good light but with an unusual color combination that makes it an excellent plant for the trough, tray, or deck box. With the right amount of sunshine, it will rebloom several times during the season.

Hosta 'Paradise on Fire'

LEAVES. Rounded, heavy substance, bright white with a wide dark green margin, 3½ × 2 in. (9 × 5 cm)

CLUMP. Upright rosette, 8 × 15 in. (20 × 38 cm)

Early morning sun will produce a steady growth rate without burning. Also ideal for the trough, window box, and the back of a small raised bed.

Hosta 'Shining Tot'

LEAVES. Oval, very thick substance, shiny dark green, 3 × 2 in. (8 × 5 cm)

CLUMP. Low, very tight, with a moderate growth rate, 5 × 15 in. (13 × 38 cm)

Prefers dappled to light shade.

The growth rate makes it an ideal plant for troughs, trays, and deck boxes.

Pipe dreams

Beyond the standard garden possibilities already mentioned, there are the non-standard, the whimsical, and the creative. In our travels, we have seen some wonderfully creative plantings of small hostas. One of the most unique was a series of upended iron pipes in the garden of Jim and Sandy Wilkins in Jackson, Michigan. Jim said he bought damaged construction-grade iron pipe that varied from 18 to 36 inches in diameter, and buried it together in the garden so that the upper ends were 12 to 36 inches above ground. The pipes were then filled with builder's sand, tamped, and topped with a mixture of builder's sand, compost, and peat. Each pipe was planted to

A group of iron pipes of various dimensions arranged at different heights and planted with little hostas in the garden of Jim and Sandy Wilkins, Jackson, Michigan.

An old galvanized wash tub, rescued from the dump and planted with a
variety of little hostas and small companion plants.

represent a slightly different type of landscape with interesting rocks, alpines, and miniature herbaceous perennials. The rusty iron complements the landscape. The rocks help the impression of terrain, and Turface (used as a mulch) blends in well with the iron.

Old wash tubs and many other types of galvanized metal containers can easily be adapted to house little hostas and other small companion plants. They can be painted bright colors or deliberately left dull. They are frost-proof and only need a number of holes drilled in the base for drainage, and they are ready to plant. If the metal container is large there is no need to fill it completely with potting soil and make it too heavy to move, even though many of them come with handles. Provided there is 4 or 5 inches of potting soil, the rest of the container can be filled with Styrofoam chips or old plastic water bottles. This idea not only reduces the weight of a large container but also greatly assists drainage.

An unusual planting: small hostas in pots hung on a house wall with wire and supported on a bamboo cane.

Clay chimney liners are meant for just that, lining a chimney. These are fired terracotta clay but not frost-proof. You can find them at building supply stores. They make attractive planters for your little hostas. Plant one small hosta in each, cut the liners to different lengths or set them into the ground at different heights. They can also support bowls. As with the iron pipes in the Wilkins garden, most of the liner can be filled with builder's sand to save on planting mix, with only the top foot devoted to the actual planting.

Hostas can even be planted in hanging planters as you would any other ornamental. Care should be taken that the pot is hung at a level where you can see the plant. June Colley and John Baker of Hampshire, England, keep their little hostas in hanging pots on the side of their house. Wire is stretched across the area, and the pots are hung at various levels, supported on bamboo poles fixed to the wall, which causes the pots to tilt slightly outward so that the plants can be admired. There are hundreds of plants arranged in this way,

When a hosta collector runs out of space, pots can be hung from a trellis, like these in the garden of June Colley and John Baker, Hampshire, England.

and it is a very clever way to display smaller hostas.

The hanging idea would also work on a decorative metal trellis. Pots can be hung at different levels—the effect is best if the pots are all similar—and the trellis either attached to a deck rail or the side of your house, or freestanding in the garden.

One less-mainstream gardening style is the world of fairy gardens, landscapes in miniature, often with whimsical ornaments to complete the impression of a place where fairies might live. In order to pull this off, plants and ornaments must be to scale. As you might expect, this genre of garden design is often created with children in mind and can be a catalyst for encouraging an early interest in gardening. Of course, there are those "young at heart" who create fairy gardens for their own amusement. Fairy gardeners sometimes claim that the garden is intended to *attract* fairies.

Fairy gardens, like miniature railroads, can be simple or very elaborate. You may have a vignette that includes a mossy path leading to a "fairy door" at the base of a tree with a potted or planted hosta to complete the illusion. Or you may stage a full village scene with small houses, pathways, streams, garden accessories, and perhaps a friendly gnome or elf for company. This is an outlet for your imagination and creativity. For those who are "craft-challenged," there are many sources for ready-

A simple fairy garden of miniature hostas planted in a round bowl.

made items to make your fantasyland come to life.

The plant material used in such a garden often is intended to represent a larger plant. For example, rosemary might be trimmed to look like a tree, or some of the easy-to-grow miniature roses might be planted for a tiny rose garden. Hostas work well in these fantasy gardens, either representing shrubbery, or representing themselves. The hostas chosen should be very small, of course, yet vigorous, especially if the garden is intended for a child, who may also find some of the names appealing.

It works! Fairies attracted to a garden of smaller hostas.

Hosta 'Rock Island Line' planted in a whimsical trough in the O'Melay garden.

Hosta 'Lakeside Elfin Fire'

LEAVES. Long and narrow, white, sometimes attractively green-flecked, with a very narrow dark green margin, 3 × 1 in. (8 × 3 cm) CLUMP. Loose and fairly upright, 5 × 10 in. (13 × 25 cm)

Although an almost white cultivar, it thrives in good light and does not easily burn. Provides excellent color contrast in any bowl of mixed hosta varieties.

Hosta 'Lakeside Small Fry'

LEAVES. Oval, pointed and slightly wavy, green with a wide creamy white edge, 3 × 2 in. (8 × 5 cm) CLUMP. Fairly fast-growing, dense, and low, 5 × 10 in. (13 × 25 cm)

Enjoys morning sun in cooler climates. Makes an excellent addition to a small hosta collection.

Hosta 'Little Willie'

LEAVES. Long and narrow, green margin and a white center that turns a streaky light green as the season progresses, 3½ × 1½ in. (9 × 4 cm)

CLUMP. Tight, slow-growing, 7 × 16 in. (18 × 40 cm)

A difficult plant to site. It needs some morning sun to look its best, but too much light will hasten the darkening of the leaves. Grows taller in deep shade. Best in a container of mixed cultivars.

Hosta 'Pixie Power'

LEAVES. Narrow, wavy and twisted, white with a bright green margin, 4 × 1½ in. (10 × 4 cm)

CLUMP. Loose and untidy, 7 × 12 in. (18 × 30 cm)

A little difficult to grow. It requires bright light but not strong sunshine to give of its best.

Hosta 'Pure Heart'

LEAVES. Rounded, white with a narrow dark green margin, 2½ × 1½ in. (6 × 4 cm)

CLUMP. A slow-growing, low rosette, 5 × 9 in. (13 × 23 cm)

Needs tender loving care when first planted. An excellent plant for the shaded rockery and fairy garden, and a fine addition to the *H.* 'Blue Mouse Ears' dynasty.

Hosta 'Tiny Tears'

LEAVES. Oval, mid-green, 3 × 2 in. (8 × 5 cm)

CLUMP. Fairly fast-growing, irregular, 5 × 18 in. (13 × 45 cm)

Ideal for almost any situation, especially as an edging plant, in a small container, or in the rockery. The most common hosta of *H. venusta* lineage, it has remained popular for more than thirty years.

Hosta 'Tot Tot'

LEAVES. Pointed and slightly wavy teardrop, blue-green, 2½ × 1½ in. (6 × 4 cm)

CLUMP. Crowded, with a moderate growth rate, 5 × 15 in. (13 × 38 cm)

Grow this tiny plant in morning sun and then dappled shade. Ideal for the rockery and fairy garden. *Hosta* 'Tet-A-Poo' is very similar.

This collection of alpine plants is enhanced by
the addition of several miniature hostas.

CHAPTER FIVE

Keeping Your Hostas Company

THERE IS NO REASON you can't grow your hostas by themselves—lots of folks do. We believe, however, that just as a good wine sets off a good meal, the right companion plants enhance your hosta garden, extending the season and enriching the experience. Furthermore, who knows? It may lead to yet a new collection.

You don't necessarily need to limit yourself to shade perennials when planning your garden. Most annuals and perennials will tolerate some shade, and most hostas will tolerate some sun. We think the more important consideration is matching the scale of the plant material to the hostas to showcase and complement them. In addition to plants, interesting rocks, garden statuary, and whimsy will make it your hosta display your own.

It's good to choose companion plants that—besides maintaining the scale you are trying to create—have cultural needs similar to the hostas. We offer some ideas that work for us.

Dwarf conifers

First of all, don't be fooled by the moniker "dwarf" when considering a conifer for a trough or vignette. A dwarf conifer simply means one that grows more slowly. Although it seems to be an oxymoron, dwarf conifers can reach 8 feet tall—not what you want to pair with your tiny hostas.

Miniature conifers are those that grow an inch or less a year, and micro-mini conifers (not a sanctioned term) are those that grow less than half an inch each year. These are the conifers that will work well with your hostas.

Like hostas, these small conifers need bright light but not sun. They require perfect drainage but good moisture (especially true of hemlocks). Choosing the right conifers to plant with your hostas will ensure your carefully planned landscape will remain balanced for years to come. Some recommended dwarf conifers follow.

Chamaecyparis obtusa (Hinoki falsecypress). The selection 'Nana' forms a dense, miniature mound that contributes beautifully to small-scale plantings, including rock gardens, troughs, and container gardens. 'Nana Lutea' is a yellow form.

Picea glauca (white spruce). The selection 'Echiniformis' is a short, cushion-growing conifer with blue-green needles. Another slow-grower, it will work in rock and container gardens as well as in your hosta bed. Looks particularly attractive with yellow hostas.

Pinus mugo (mugo pine). 'Little Delight' is a nice, small, rounded selection of mugo pine.

Tsuga canadensis (Canadian hemlock). Hemlocks enjoy the same conditions as your little hostas: moist but well-drained soil. They will tolerate more shade than other conifers and tend to grow more slowly, 1 to 2 inches per year. Two dwarf selections of Canadian hemlock are worth seeking out. 'Stewart's Gem' forms a flattened mound; the tiny leaves are borne on branches with cinnamon-brown tips. 'Stockman's Dwarf' is a wider than tall dwarf with flat, layered branches covered in deep green needles.

Smaller trees and shrubs

Smaller trees and shrubs provide valuable shade for your hostas, particularly welcome in the understory of a woodland garden, adding both texture and interest.

Japanese maples (*Acer palmatum*) do well in shadier gardens, and their lacy foliage will be kind to the light requirements of your hostas (remembering that hostas are shade-tolerant, not shade-loving). Their often deeply dissected leaves, especially, echo the scale of the plants sited beneath them. Japanese maples, even the dwarfs, will eventually grow to 6 feet or more, so make sure to do your research and plant with the mature height in mind.

Acer palmatum 'Fairy Hair' is an oddball, tiny little Japanese maple with curling threadlike leaves, unlike any other you're likely to find.

Acer palmatum 'Goshiki-kotohime' is a dwarf, variegated form of 'Kotohime'. The new spring growth is often pink, speckled with red, yellow, white, and green. Summer

A hypertufa tray of little hostas, with added interest provided by a piece of miniature sculpture.

color is a rich green with differing amounts of variegation.

Acer palmatum 'Sharp's Pygmy'. The tiny leaves on this dwarf Japanese maple are quite nice. A deep green summer color gives way to oranges for the fall display. Slow-growing and densely branched.

Shrubs and trees that have been downsized can work with even your smallest hostas. For a more formal look, there are small boxwoods that can be trimmed as you would a larger variety. For example, *Buxus microphylla* 'Morris Midget' is a very small selection with evergreen leaves; it can be pruned to create tiny topiary or hedging, or left to grow as a loose globe.

Buxus microphylla 'Kingsville', another recommended boxwood selection, is tiny and slow-growing.

Euonymus japonicus 'Microphyllus Pulchellus' (golden dwarf boxleaf euonymus) is an easy-to-grow plant that can be trimmed into a small hedge.

Ginkgo biloba 'Troll' is a delightful little version of the ancient tree.

Small hostas with miniature conifers.

A mixed planting in a simple glazed bowl: joining one green and two variegated hostas, a small Japanese maple adds some height, and a tatting fern adds a different texture and breaks up the edge of the container.

Ilex crenata 'Dwarf Pagoda' (dwarf Japanese holly) holds its tiny, dark green glossy leaves on irregular branches. This holly grows only 2 inches per year, so is very suitable for containers.

Pieris japonica 'Little Heath Green' and *P.j.* 'Little Heath Variegata' are small compact flowering shrubs with shiny leaves. New growth is blushed pink.

Mosses, ferns, and other shade-tolerant companions

Mosses should not be overlooked as a partner to smaller hostas—especially when you are considering a small world, a world up close, a contemplative world. Moss works well in such a setting and will tie it all together if you are going for a woodland look. Ferns do well in woodland, too, and provide a wonderful busy contrast to simple hosta foliage. But there are additional shade-tolerant plants and bulbs to consider to keep your little hostas company. Some of our favorites follow.

Arisaema (Jack in the pulpit). A genus of plants that are enjoying a sharply upward trajectory of popularity. Some varieties are quite large and will overwhelm your little hostas. Stick with smaller selections of *Aa. flavum* and *sikokianum*.

Astilbe 'Sprite' and others of the new dwarf

A ghost fern (*Athyrium* 'Ghost') planted beside *Hosta* 'Grand Prize' provides contrast of both color and form.

astilbes now available on the market will bring color to the hosta garden, especially a garden with more shade, with their foamy spikes of delicate pastel blooms.

Brunnera macrophylla (Siberian bugloss). There are many new and colorful selections of this species available today. Although some of them grow a little large, they are ideal plants to fill the back of a woodland bed or walk and provide good color and form contrast to foreground hostas. 'Jack Frost' is one of the best new selections.

Corydalis. For ages, the only species available was *C. lutea*, and while the ferny foliage and dependable yellow all-season blooms were welcome, they were also boring. Now there are all kinds of variations—some with white, pink, or blue flowers, some with blue foliage. Our favorite has to be *C.* 'Berry Exciting': the foliage is bright gold, the spring flowers are lavender-purple, and the effect is stunning.

Cyclamen coum. An exotic hardy bulb (corm) that sends up the most outrageously patterned foliage in late summer and flowers

Brunnera macrophylla 'Jack Frost' with *Hosta* 'Bob Olson'.

through the winter, going dormant in the heat of the summer. They need to be in drier shade, which is usually easy to provide.

Dicentra (bleeding heart) is another genus that has been subject to dwarfing, courtesy of avid hybridizers. The ferny foliage looks good even when plants are not blooming.

Disporum (fairy bells) is a genus of wonderful companions for little hostas. Some species form gently arching wands like Solomon's seal; others arrange themselves in tight clumps, looking more like lilies of the valley.

Another collectible plant to deplete your mad money.

Epimedium (barrenwort) is a genus that has become more and more mainstream, and its members will beautifully complement your smallest hosta. These are low-growing herbaceous perennials with spidery flowers that are best appreciated on hands and knees—or in a raised bed with your choicest little hostas. Some epimediums, like *E. grandiflorum* var. *higoense* 'Bandit', have showy foliage as well. Some spread to form a polite groundcover, but

The bright ferny foliage of *Corydalis* 'Berry Exciting' and lobelias in bloom punctuate this window box, filled to overflowing with *Hosta* 'Junior Miss', *H.* 'Midnight Moon', *H.* 'Bob Olson', and *H.* 'Quarter Note'.

many remain in a delicate clump. They too are worth collecting.

Hedera (ivy). We have rock walls in our garden. Ivy does not have the best reputation because it can be a thug. You would certainly not use it as a living mulch for your little hostas, but for draping gracefully over a rock wall, we defy you to find a better plant. *Hedera helix* (English ivy) is common. There are more interesting offerings with deeply cut leaves, some with white frosting and some with yellow variegation. Hardiness can be an issue in cooler climates (and invasiveness in warmer), so check before planting.

Heuchera is another "hula hoop" genus where hybridizing gone wild has provided endless cultivars. For our purposes, we recommend the harder-to-find petites such as *H.* 'Petite Pearl Fairy' and *H.* 'Petite Marbled Burgundy'. Happily, hucheras grow best with the same drainage and light requirements as little hostas.

Hydrangea anomala subsp. *petiolaris* (climbing hydrangea). A climbing hydrangea is one

Heuchera 'Peach Flame' contrasts nicely with this streamside planting of hostas, including *H.* 'Limey Lisa' and *H.* 'Twist of Lime'.

of those plants that will test your patience—it sleeps, it creeps, it leaps. It will take time to establish, three years, maybe longer, but have faith—you won't be sorry. Climbing hydrangeas, mini or otherwise, are not particular about soil, and they prefer some shade, but they do take their sweet time settling in. They will offer vertical interest in your woodland. Let them climb up a tall stump or sturdy tree.

Narcissus (daffodil). The woodland garden awakens in the spring in waves. You can keep the excitement going from early spring until late fall by planting dwarf daffodils and other minor bulbs, such as autumn crocus (*Colchicum*), as companions for your little hostas. Among the best of the many dwarf daffodils available on the market are N. 'Tête-à-Tête', with tiny cheerful yellow flowers, and N. 'Minnow', white and yellow. Both are small and very early, reliable bloomers. The down side—an important caveat—is that, as with all daffodils, the foliage will need to remain in place long after the flower is done blooming, which may spoil the look of your garden unless you

This tiny tray is crammed with ferns, oxalis, and small hostas.

Hosta 'Cracker Crumbs', emerging in spring through a living mulch of wild violets.

carefully plan for disguising it. Other small bulbs that we enjoy include squill (*Scilla*), a lovely blue, early spring bulb that readily naturalizes, and snowdrops (*Galanthus*), extra early white blooms, often blooming through the snow in our garden, that will politely go dormant before your hostas fully leaf out.

Primula (primrose). There are countless species, selections, and hybrids of primulas, from the cheerful tall rosy shades of *P. japonica*, to the lovely yellow *P. vulgaris*, to the day-glo supermarket *P. ×polyantha*. Most primulas are carefree and excellent companions to your hostas. In warmer, drier climates, cut back the leaves in the stressful months of midsummer to conserve moisture; they will regrow their leaves in the cool of the autumn.

Tiarella (foamflower). Another collectible plant. The number of cultivars is dizzying, but not all share the same vigor. These can be either running or clump-forming, low plants with lobed foliage, some with striking dark patterns. The flowers are bottlebrush style and range from white to pastel pink. Foamflowers tolerate quite heavy shade.

Trillium, a genus of native American wildflowers (also native to parts of Asia), is at home in the woodland garden, and when acclimated, species like *T. grandiflorum* will form an early spring carpet of white.

Viola (violet) can be a thug, so choose your companions carefully. Some modern cultivars are grown for their foliage; one such is *V.* 'Mars', which has stunning red markings on its foliage.

Hosta 'Golden Tiara', the original
sport from a species hosta.

CHAPTER SIX
Collecting Hostas

ONE OF THE FASCINATING attributes of hostas is their propensity to morph into a new variety, or sport. In such cases, a parent plant develops new leaves unlike the rest of the plant. Maybe there is a wider leaf edge or a lighter leaf center. In fact, there are cases where the sport is totally unlike the original plant, with reversed variegation or a different color pattern altogether.

Often when a hosta sports and the new plant is worthy of naming, the grower will link it to the original in choosing a new cultivar name. Some hostas have many sports attributed to them, and we will describe some of these series, or "dynasties," here.

One quick notation on these dynasties: although the appearance of the hosta may change, the basic cultural requirements do not, so that if you can grow one well, the same care should enable you to grow the rest in the series just as well.

Tiara/Scepter Series
Probably the most famous dynasty of small hostas is the Tiara/Scepter Series. *Hosta* 'Golden Tiara' (a 1977 Robert Savory introduction) was the first in the series, and it is interesting to note that this original plant was itself a sport from a species (either *Hh. nakaiana* or *capitata*—the origin is disputed). *Hosta* 'Golden Tiara' is still very popular, widely available, and grown in many gardens today. The plant is registered as growing to 12 inches high and forms a nice organized clump of green, oval to heart-shaped leaves with a narrow gold margin. It blooms profusely with neat purple flowers centered in the mound like a bouquet. Although the leaves are somewhat lacking in substance, the overall plant is sturdy and vigorous and will grow happily in most gardens without special attention.

The first naturally occurring sport that sprang from *H.* 'Golden Tiara', also introduced by Savory, was *H.* 'Golden Scepter', an all-yellow version of *H.* 'Golden Tiara' that enjoys the same vigor and profuse flowering.

Micropropagation, or tissue culturing (TC), accelerated the rate at which hosta sports occur. Thanks to this process, many sports of *H.* 'Golden Tiara' followed.

Sports of *Hosta* 'Golden Tiara'

• *Hosta* 'Diamond Tiara', the first variegated sport of *H.* 'Golden Tiara', is green with a white margin.

• *Hosta* 'Emerald Scepter'. A reverse-variegated sport, yellow with a narrow green margin.

• *Hosta* 'Floral Tiara'. Similar to *H.* 'Golden Tiara' but with flowers twice the size and held at a 90 degree angle to the scape.

• *Hosta* 'Glen Tiara'. A small mound of gold-edged, green-centered foliage, similar but smaller than the original.

• *Hosta* 'Grand Tiara'. A polyploid sport with a wide yellow margin, feathered green center, and much heavier leaf substance.

• *Hosta* 'Jade Scepter'. Fully green and very vigorous.

• *Hosta* 'Ribbon Tiara'. A sport with an unusually narrow green center.

• *Hosta* 'Streaked Tiara'. A streaked sport.

• *Hosta* 'Sunny Tiara'. Very closely resembles *H.* 'Golden Scepter'.

• *Hosta* 'Touchstone'. Green with narrow white margin, strongly similar to *H.* 'Diamond Tiara'.

But wait, there's more. *Hosta* 'Golden Tiara' passed another trait along to its progeny along with vigor: the propensity to sport. Leaf shape and profuse flowering are passed along, although the leaves and plant may be smaller.

Two members of the Tiara/Scepter dynasty, *H.* 'Golden Scepter' and *H.* 'Grand Tiara'.

Hosta 'Diamond Tiara'

Hosta 'Emerald Scepter'

Sports of sports of *Hosta* 'Golden Tiara'

- *Hosta* 'Emerald Tiara'. From *H.* 'Golden Scepter', golden with a green margin.

- *Hosta* 'Lime Tiara'. From *H.* 'Emerald Scepter', light green foliage.

- *Hosta* 'Margaret Mary Tiara'. From *H.* 'Diamond Tiara', wide white margin that sometimes streaks into the mid- to dark green center.

- *Hosta* 'Opal Scepter'. From *H.* 'Golden Scepter', gold with creamy white and yellow streaks.

- *Hosta* 'Pearl Tiara'. From *H.* 'Diamond Tiara', slightly smaller and less vigorous, with a wider margin.

- *Hosta* 'Platinum Tiara'. From *H.* 'Golden Scepter', golden with a thin white margin.

- *Hosta* 'Royal Tiara'. From *H.* 'Jade Scepter', white with a wider green margin. The white center causes the leaves to twist in an interesting manner; however, some of the vigor associated with the rest of the dynasty is absent here.

- *Hosta* 'Russian Tiara'. From *H.* 'Diamond Tiara', deep green with a creamy white to goldish green margin.

- *Hosta* 'Silver Tiara'. From *H.* 'Golden Scepter', white with a narrow light green margin.

Some of the sports throw off just as many variations as the original. *Hosta* 'Grand Tiara', with its extra chromosomes, has a mini-

Hosta 'Touchstone'

Hosta 'Emerald Tiara'

Hosta 'Platinum Tiara'

dynasty of its own (here and henceforth presented in order of registration). The difference in *these* plants is the increased substance due to the polyploid nature of the original plant.

Sports of *Hosta* 'Grand Tiara'

• *Hosta* 'Gilded Tiara'. Chartreuse with a very narrow yellow margin.

• *Hosta* 'Ivory Tiara'. Green with a white margin.

• *Hosta* 'Amber Tiara'. All yellow, sometimes showing small green flecking.

• *Hosta* 'Crystal Tiara'. Vivid yellow, fading to white, with a bright green margin. Not as strong a grower.

• *Hosta* 'Gold Heart'. The reverse of original: bright gold with a bright green margin.

• *Hosta* 'Grand Gold'. Unregistered and very similar to *H.* 'Amber Tiara'.

• *Hosta* 'Grand Prize'. Bright green with a wide lemon-yellow margin that fades to white later in the season.

• *Hosta* 'Heavenly Tiara'. Light green with a yellow-feathered margin that fades to white as the season progresses.

• *Hosta* 'Topaz Tiara'. Wide green margin feathering into a yellow center.

As time marches on, there have been yet more Tiaras and Scepters; for example, *H.*

Hosta 'Royal Tiara'

Hosta 'Heavenly Tiara'

Hosta 'Topaz Tiara'

'Amber Tiara' begat both *H.* 'Binkie' (described in chapter four) and *H.* 'Flame Tiara', with a heavily rippled greenish yellow margin and a creamy white center streaked yellow. Most are quite rare and difficult to find. Still, it's easy to see where the sporting life can lead!

Baby Bunting Series

Hosta 'Baby Bunting', the original plant in this series, is a hybrid—that is, a hosta that occurred as the result of cross-pollination between two hostas. A tiny blue, it is nevertheless an excellent plant and will hold its own in the garden. Although it is sterile, *H.* 'Baby Bunting' has brought us some of the most famous of the smallest hostas through sporting.

• *Hosta* 'Pandora's Box'. From *H.* 'Baby Bunting' and a sensation among collectors upon its 1996 introduction: here was a stunning little plant, carrying the blue-green margin from *H.* 'Baby Bunting', but with a striking white center on each leaf. Reversions are common in sports, and *H.* 'Pandora's Box' is notorious. Remove fully green leaves quickly, or you will find yourself with *H.* 'Baby Bunting' where *H.* 'Pandora's Box' once grew.

• *Hosta* 'Hope'. Mid-green with a wide gold edge, the first sport of *H.* 'Pandora's Box'.

• *Hosta* 'Cameo'. A sport from *H.* 'Baby Bunting' and the reverse of *H.* 'Pandora's Box', green-blue with an irregular creamy white margin. Easy to grow.

• *Hosta* 'Cherish'. Another *H.* 'Baby Bunting' sport, creamy yellow with a wide blue-green margin. The center will gradually fade to white by midsummer.

Cheatin Heart Series

Hosta 'Cheatin Heart' (described in chapter four) spawned a series of hostas that tell a tale, like the country song for which the plant was named. Again, the size of the sports shift, but not the basic "bones" of the plant.

• *Hosta* 'Change of Heart'. Pale yellow, a wide white edge, and a green pattern shadowing the border between the two primary colors.

• *Hosta* 'Faithful Heart'. Gold with a narrow green margin.

• *Hosta* 'Illicit Affair'. Mid-green with a bright yellow margin.

• *Hosta* 'Stolen Kiss'. A golden center with a narrow green edge.

• *Hosta* 'Heart Broken'. Emerges gold and fades to green later in the season.

And the sports carry on. *Hosta* 'Silver Threads and Golden Needles', a sport from *H.* 'Stolen Kiss', is a lovely affair (you should pardon the pun) glimpsed in chapter four. Its name seems not to fit the series, but if you go back to the country song roots of *H.* 'Cheatin Heart', you'll find the lyrics refer to mending a broken heart.

Lemon Lime Series

Hosta 'Lemon Lime' (described in chapter four) is a vigorous grower and prolific sporter; it may even rebloom if the first flower stalks are removed before setting seed. It can be a thug in a trough or in a small vignette if not kept in check by frequent dividing; conversely, if you need a plant for lining a path or groundcover,

H. 'Lemon Lime' will happily comply in a few short seasons.

All its sports have proved to be as vigorous as the original, although as with many sports, they vary in size.

• *Hosta* 'Lemon Delight'. A miniature with gold margin and a green center. Grow in good light for best leaf contrast.

• *Hosta* 'Lemon Frost'. Chartreuse center, white margin.

• *Hosta* 'Lemon Sorbet'. Another miniature, rippled leaves with a greenish yellow center and a white margin.

• *Hosta* 'Lime Meringue'. Rippled leaves, mid-green with a pure white margin.

• *Hosta* 'Twist of Lime'. Yellow with green margin.

Notable in the second generation is *H.* 'Iced Lemon', a sport of *H.* 'Lemon Delight' with white-margined yellow-green leaves.

Hosta 'Faithful Heart'

Hosta 'Lemon Frost'

Hosta 'Twist of Lime'

Mouse Ears Series

Hosta 'Blue Mouse Ears', described in chapter four and the originator of the series, is another hosta that immediately caught the attention of collectors. It is an excellent small plant with much to recommend it: very heavy substance, proportional and vigorous growth habits, and a *very* cute name. It is also one of those wonderfully unstable plants that has already given us a proliferation of sports, with many more possible.

• *Hosta* 'Blue Mouse Ears Supreme'. A streaked version, which means that the blue-green base is shot through with lighter streaks—yellow and cream, in this case.

• *Hosta* 'Cat and Mouse'. A variegated sport, greenish yellow with a feathered blue-green margin.

• *Hosta* 'Green Mouse Ears'. A green sport, maintaining the heavy substance, cute round leaves, and proportional flower stalks of the original.

• *Hosta* 'Mighty Mouse'. Blue-green with a pale yellow margin that turns to white later in the season.

• *Hosta* 'Royal Mouse Ears'. Blue-green base, streaked gold.

• *Hosta* 'Snow Mouse'. White with a blue-green margin.

• *Hosta* 'One Iota'. Dark green with a creamy edge.

Hosta 'Iced Lemon'

• *Hosta* 'Mouse Trap'. A miniature, bright white with a blue-green margin.

And when the sports sport? The next generation . . .

Sports of sports of *Hosta* 'Blue Mouse Ears'

Hosta 'Holy Mouse Ears'. From *H.* 'Royal Mouse Ears', creamy white with a feathered blue-green margin.

Hosta 'One Iota Streaked'. From *H.* 'One Iota', blue-green, streaked creamy white.

Hosta 'Frosted Mouse Ears'. From *H.* 'Royal Mouse Ears', thick blue leaves with a wide creamy margin that fades to white as the season progresses.

Hosta 'Mouse Tracks'. Streaked version of *H.* 'Mighty Mouse'.

Hosta 'Pure Heart'. From *H.* 'Mighty Mouse' (and named for his best gal, Pearl Pureheart), creamy white center, dark green margin.

Forming collections is a fun, not to say addictive, aspect of growing hostas. The groups we are calling "dynasties" can be the basis of a

Some members of the *Hosta* 'Blue Mouse Ears' dynasty planted together in a ceramic tray.

collection (we've even seen one Mouse Ears Series group planting, taken to the extreme, that included porcelain mice and a hunk of ceramic cheese); but collections are often based on plant *names* instead of a sporting connection. A gardener may seek out fairy or fantasy names (e.g., *H.* 'Imp', *H.* 'Pixie Vamp', *H.* 'Dragon Tails'), names containing cat references (e.g., *H.* 'Cat's Eye', *H.* 'Kitty Cat', *H.* 'Cat and Mouse'), or food names (e.g., *H.* 'Coconut Custard', *H.* 'Lakeside Lollipop').

One of the most gratifying elements of planning a collection, whether based on a sport connection or a name connection, is in identifying a desirable plant and then hunting it down. Some plants are readily available; some are rare and difficult to obtain. We keep a "wish list" of targets that must be located. It's a lovely satisfying feeling to tick a plant off the list. We sincerely hope we have encouraged you to start a new collection and experience the same.

Hosta 'Mouse Tracks'

Hosta 'Frosted Mouse Ears'

Sources

Hostas

Belgium
Danny van Eechaute
Joos Vijdtdreef 16
9800 Dienze
www.hostacollectie.be

Canada
Goldenbrook Hostas
14950 Regional Rd. 57
Blackstock, ON L0B 1B0
www.goldenbrookhostas.com

Olde Towne Gardens
716 Lakeshore Rd.
Niagara-on-the-Lake, ON
   L0S 1J0
www.oldetownegardens.ca

Rideau Woodland Ramble
Box 348
Merrickville, ON K0G 1N0
www.rideauwoodlandramble.
   com/

Shades of Green
48855 John Wise Line
Aylmer, ON N5H 2R4
http://www.shades-of-green.
   ca/

France
Le Jardin Anglais
Cantiran
47230 Montgaillard
www.lejardinanglais.com

Germany
Friesland-Staudengarten
Husumerweg 16
26441 Jever/Rahdum
www.friesland-staudengar-
   ten.de

Netherlands
Fransen Hostas
Paradijsweg 5
2461 TK Ter Aar
www.hostaparadise.com

Hostaworld B.V.
Wesselseweg 46
3771 PC Barneveld
www.hostaworld.nl

New Zealand
Taunton Gardens
Allandale, RD 1
Lyttleton, Christchurch
www.tauntongardens.co.nz

United Kingdom
Apple Court
Hordle, Lymington
Hampshire SO14 0HU
www.applecourt.com

Bali-Hai Nursery
42 Largy Road, Carnlough
Ballymena, Co.Antrim
Northern Ireland BT44 0EZ
www.mailorderplants4me.
   com

Bowden Hostas
Sticklepath
Okehampton
Devon EX20 2NL
www.bowdenhostas.com

Brookfield Plants
Bigelle, Sandyhurst Lane
Ashford
Kent TN25 4NX
www.brookfieldplants.com

Goldbrook Plants
Hoxne, Eye
Suffolk IP21 5AN

Mary Green
The Walled Garden
Hornby, nr. Lancaster
Lancashire
marygreenplants@aol.com

Hutton Hostas
Howl Lane, Hutton, Driffield
East Yorkshire YO25 9QD
www.huttonhostas.com

Loch-Hills Plant Centre
Ava Macgregor
Ellon, Aberdeen
info@loch-hillsplants.co.uk

Mickfield Hostas
Mickfield, Stowmarket
Suffolk IP14 5LH
www.mickfieldhostas.co.uk

Park Green Nurseries
Wetheringsett, Stowmarket
Suffolk, IP14 5QH
www.parkgreen.co.uk

United States
Azalea Patch
2010 Mountain Rd.
Joppa, MD 21085
www.azaleapatch.com

Bloomin Designs Nursery
558 Auburn Rd.
Auburn, GA 30011
www.bloomindesigns.com

Carlson's Gardens
Box 305, 26 Salem Hill Rd.
South Salem, NY 10590
www.carlsonsgardens.com

Daylily and Hosta Gardens
2396 Roper Mountain Rd.
Simpsonville, SC 29681
www.daylilyandhostagardens.
   com

Eagle Bay Gardens
10749 Bennett Rd.
Dunkirk, NY 14048
www.eaglebaygardens.com

Glenbrook Farms
142 Brooks Rd.
Fultonville, NY 12072
www.glenbrookplants.com

Green Hill Hostas
Box 16306
Chapel Hill, NC 27516
www.hostahosta.com

Hilltop Farm
3307 N State Hwy F
Ash Grove, MO 65604
www.hilltop-gardens.com

Honey Hill Hostas
3633 Honey Hill Dr. SE
Cedar Rapids, IA 52403-1919
www.hosta-holic.com

Hornbaker Gardens
22937 1140 N. Ave.
Princeton, IL 61356
www.hornbakergardens.com

Hosta Homestead
9448 Mayfield Rd.
Chesterland, OH 44026-2259
www.hostahomestead.com

Hosta Patch
23720 Hearthside Dr.
Deer Park, IL 60010
www.hostapatch.com

Jim's Hostas
11676 Robinhood Dr.
Dubuque, IA 52001
www.jimshostas.com

Klehm's Song Sparrow
13101 East Rye Rd.
Avalon, WI 53505
www.songsparrow.com

Kuk's Forest Nursery
10174 Barr Rd.
Brecksville, OH 44141
www.gardensights.com/kuks/
    index.html

Lee's Gardens
25986 Sauder Rd.
Tremont, IL 61568
www.leesgardens.com

Made in the Shade Gardens
16370 W. 138th Terrace
Olathe, KS 66062
www.hostaguy.com

Naylor Creek Nursery
Box 309
Chimacum, WA 98325
www.naylorcreek.com

New Hampshire Hostas
73 Exeter Rd.
South Hampton, NH 03827
www.nhhostas.com

Oakcrest Gardens
22871 Kane Ave.
Glenwood, IA 51534
www.oakcrestgardens.com

O'Brien Nurserymen
40 Wells Rd.
Granby, CT 06035
www.obrienhosta.com

Pine Forest Gardens
556 Ellison Rd.
Tyrone, GA 30290-1804
www.pineforestgardens.com

Plant Delights Nursery
9241 Sauls Rd.
Raleigh, NC 27603
www.plantdelights.com

Savory's Gardens
5300 Whiting Ave.
Edina, MN 55439
www.savorysgardens.com

Schmid Nursery and
    Gardens
847 Westwood Boulevard
Jackson, MI 49203
www.schmidgardens.com

Sebright Gardens
Box 9058
Brooks, OR 97305
www.sebrightgardens.com

Silvers-Elbert Nursery
2024 McDaniel Mill Rd.
Conyers, GA 30207
www.hostaplants.com

Soules Garden
5809 Rahke Rd.
Indianapolis, IN 46217
www.soulesgarden.com

Wade and Gatton Nurseries
1288 Gatton Rocks Rd.
Bellville, OH 44813
www.wadeandgattonnurser-
    ies.com

Walnut Grove Nursery
8348 E State Rd. 45
Unionville, IN 47468
www.walnutgrovenursery.net

White Oak Nursery
1 Oak Park Lane
Metamora, IL 61548
www.whiteoaknursery.com

Shade and companion plants

Arrowhead Alpines
1310 North Gregory Rd.
Fowlerville, MI 48836
www.arrowheadalpines.com
Extensive collection of rare and choice plants,
   all types

Garden Vision Epimediums
Box 50
Templeton, MA 01468
www.home.earthlink.net/~darrellpro/
Epimediums and other shade perennials, free
   catalog upon request

Oriental Garden Supply
448 W. Bloomfield Rd.
Pittsford, NY 14534
www.orientalgardensupply.com/
Specializing in Japanese maples, dwarf coni-
   fers, and bonsai supplies

Mulberry Creek Herb Farm
3312 Bogart Rd.
Huron, OH 44839
http://mulberrycreek.com/
Specializing in small and miniature plants,
   fairy gardens

Where to See Little Hostas

In addition to the hosta suppliers listed, many of whom maintain stocks and sometimes collections of little hostas, the following individuals have collections of smaller hostas that may be viewed by appointment only.

Europe

Diana Grenfell, Newnham-on-Severn, Gloucestershire, England
Holder of the National Plant Collection of Very Small and Miniature Hostas
diana@uppermerton.co.uk

Jonathan Hogarth, Wokingham, Berkshire, England
ahogie25@aol.com

Ian Scroggy, Ballymena, Northern Ireland
balihainursery@btinternet.com

June Colley and John Baker, Lindford, Hampshire, England
hanginghostas@tesco.net

Hugo Philips, Belgium
Hugo.Philips@skynet.be

United States

Barbara and Robert Tiffany, Point Pleasant, Pennsylvania
btiffany@comcast.net

Eve and Per Thyrum, Wilmington, Delaware
evethyrum1@comcast.net

Toni Wright, Decatur, Georgia
toniw@bellsouth.net

Kathy Guest Shadrack and Michael Shadrack, Hamburg, New York
irisborer@aol.com

Further Reading

British Hosta and Hemerocallis Society Bulletin, www.hostahem.org.uk (British Hosta and Hemerocallis Society)

The Complete Shade Gardener by George Schenk (Houghton Mifflin)

Gardening with Woodland Plants by Karan Junker (Timber Press)

The Genus Hosta and *An Encyclopedia of Shade Perennials*, both by W. George Schmid (Timber Press)

Green Hill Gossip, published by Bob Solberg, www.hostahosta.com

Hosta Finder, published by Steve Greene, shgreene@aol.com

Hosta: The Flowering Foliage Plant by Diana Grenfell (Timber Press)

The Hosta Handbook and *The Hostapedia*, both by Mark R. Zilis (Q & Z Nursery, Inc.)

The Hosta Journal, published by the American Hosta Society, www.americanhostasociety.org/

Hosta Library, www.hostalibrary.org

Hosta Registry, www.hostaregistrar.org

Hostas by Diana Grenfell (RHS Wisley Handbooks)

Hosta Valley by Jeroen Linneman, www.hostavalley.eu

Mini Hosta Forum, http://groups.yahoo.com/group/minihosta

My Hostas Database, by Hugo Philips, http://myhostas.be

The Natural Shade Garden by Ken Druse (Clarkson-Potter)

The New Color Encyclopedia of Hostas and *Timber Press Pocket Guide to Hostas*, both by Diana Grenfell and Michael Shadrack (Timber Press)

Index